D1191816

2

Ataque de Modismos

Idiom

Attack

1 Everyday Living

Peter N. Liptak

Peter N. Liptak came to Asia in 1995 to teach English, then started learning Korean and working as a writer and copywriter. As a poet and teacher of English, his desire to help people around the globe in their struggles with the untamed beauty of the English language has led to teaching at universities and the writing of language acquisition books. After finishing a Master's in Korean Studies at Yonsei University, Peter involved himself with several other writing projects including a series of children's books, a translation of Korean poetry into English and a website helping foreign nationals to become acclimated to Korea and its culture. Currently, Peter enjoys exploring the world while training for triathlons, mountain biking, and competing in ultra-marathons while raising money for orphans to experience outdoor activities.

Peter N. Liptak se trasladó a Asia en 1995 para enseñar inglés. Luego, comenzó a aprender coreano y a trabajar como escritor y redactor de textos. Como poeta y profesor de inglés, su deseo por ayudar a la gente en su lucha con la indomable belleza del idioma inglés lo ha llevado a enseñar en universidades y a escribir libros de adquisición de idiomas. Concluida su maestría en Estudios Coreanos en la Universidad de Yonsei, Peter está abocado ahora a varios otros proyectos entre los que se encuentra la elaboración de una serie de libros infantiles, la traducción al inglés de poesía coreana, así como la preparación de un sitio web para ayudar a ciudadanos extranjeros a habituarse a Corea y a su cultura. En la actualidad, Peter disfruta de explorar el mundo mientras se entrena para participar en triatlones, ciclismo de montaña y ultramaratones, al mismo tiempo que recauda dinero para que los huérfanos puedan disfrutar actividades al aire libre.

Matthew Douma

Matthew Douma grew up in a small rural town in Southern Canada. Ever since his early childhood years, Matthew has had a deep interest in Asia and made his first visit when he was just fifteen years old. As an avid outdoorsman and adventurer, Matthew enjoys sports of all sorts including Taekwondo. Matthew also has a passion for mountain climbing, sailing and writing as hobbies. Residing in Seoul with his lovely wife Sun Hee and daughter Ennik, he works as an English education consultant and author of English educational material.

Matthew Douma creció en un pequeño pueblo rural al sur de Canadá. Desde sus primeros años, demostró un profundo interés en Asia y realizó su primera visita a la corta edad de quince años. Como ávido entusiasta del aire libre y de las aventuras, Matthew disfruta de toda clase de deporte, entre los que se incluye el taekwondo. También tiene pasatiempos apasionantes como el montañismo, la navegación a vela y la escritura. Matthew trabaja como consultor educativo y autor de material educativo para la enseñanza del idioma inglés mientras reside en Seúl con su encantadora esposa Sun Hee y su hija Ennik.

Jay Douma

An elementary school teacher since 1999, Jay enjoys writing stories and collaborating with his brother on creative projects. Currently teaching grade five and physical education in Ontario, Canada, Jay enjoys spending time with his wife Christa and daughter Emma at their home on Lake Erie when not working.

Maestro de escuela primaria desde 1999, Jay gusta de escribir historias y de colaborar con su hermano en proyectos creativos. En la actualidad, enseña el quinto grado y educación física en Ontario, Canadá. Cuando no está trabajando, Jay disfruta de pasar el tiempo con su esposa Christa y su hija Emma en su casa del lago Erie.

* A bow to our translator Un reconocimiento para nuestro traductor

Patricia Urbano became interested in languages as an early teenager. After finishing her studies at an Italian High School, she entered Ricardo Palma University in Peru. In 1995, she got a degree in Spanish Translation and two years later, she joined the Peruvian Translators Association as a pioneer member. She works in Peru as a translator from English, French, Italian and Portuguese into Spanish.

Patricia Urbano se mostró interesada en los idiomas desde sus primeros años de adolescencia. Luego de terminar sus estudios secundarios en un colegio italiano, ingresó a la Universidad Ricardo Palma en Perú. En 1995, obtuvo el título de Licenciada en Traducción y dos años más tarde se hizo miembro del Colegio de Traductores del Perú. Patricia trabaja en Lima como traductora de inglés, francés, italiano y portugués al español.

Ataque de Modismos

Idiom

Attack

1 **Everyday Living**

por Peter, Matthew y Jay

Getting Used to Idioms

Conquering idioms – A three-step training process

Idioms decorate the daily conversations of native English speakers in various ways. An idiom is a phrase in which two or more words come together to create a unique meaning that is different from the meaning of each of the individual words. Because the combination of words will seem peculiar to non-native speakers, it is quite difficult for foreigners to learn idioms. If your goal is to conquer English, you must conquer idioms (before they attack you).

This book includes about 300 frequently used idioms divided into 25 thematic chapters. The themes are key topics of English conversation used in daily life and business, for describing actions and expressing emotions. Each chapter introduces 10-15 idioms. The meaning of each idiom is explained in both English and Spanish. Example sentences help your understanding and use of the idioms. And to enable in-depth learning, this book includes a story that uses the idioms introduced in each chapter.

Step 1. Learn the meaning of idioms through Spanish
Infer the meaning of the idioms inserted into Spanish sentences, and then take a look at how the idioms are used in example English sentences. This is an easier and more effective way to learn their meaning and use. In addition, the idioms are used in the Spanish sentence to help you recall them.

Step 2. Confirm the use of idioms with the fill-in-the-blank section
Confirm the meaning of the idioms once again by filling in the blanks in additional example sentences. A translation right below each sentence and one or two words in the idiom presented as a clue enable you to easily complete the sentences and completely familiarize yourself with the idioms.

Step 3. Practice the use of the idioms by reading a story
Each of the short, but interesting stories enables you to understand how idioms are used in real-life settings. You can increase your skill with idioms and even start to sound like a native speaker by practicing the story and answering the questions.

Conquista los modismos – Un método de tres pasos

Los modismos adornan las conversaciones cotidianas de los hablantes nativos de inglés de diversas maneras. Un modismo es una frase en la que dos o más palabras se unen para crear un significado único, diferente al significado de cada una de las palabras individuales. Debido a que los hablantes no nativos encuentran extraña la combinación de palabras, a los extranjeros les es muy difícil aprender los modismos. Si tu objetivo es dominar el inglés, debes dominar los modismos (antes de que estos te ataquen).

Este libro incluye cerca de 300 modismos de uso frecuente divididos en 25 capítulos temáticos. Los temas son puntos claves de conversación que se usan en la vida diaria y los negocios para describir acciones y expresar emociones. Cada capítulo presenta entre 10 y 15 modismos, los cuales se explican con ejemplos tanto en inglés como en español para facilitar su uso y comprensión. Además, el libro incluye una historia donde se emplean los modismos que aparecen en cada capítulo.

Primer paso. Aprende el significado de los modismos mediante el español
Deduce el significado de los modismos insertados en las oraciones en español y luego observa la manera en que se utilizan en los ejemplos en inglés. Esto te permitirá aprender su uso y significado de una manera más fácil y eficaz. Además, los modismos se emplean en las oraciones en español para que los recuerdes con mayor facilidad.

Segundo paso. Refuerza el uso de los modismos con la sección para completar
Refuerza el significado de los modismos al llenar los espacios en blanco en otros ejemplos. Podrás completar las oraciones con facilidad y familiarizarte completamente con los modismos gracias a que encontrarás la traducción debajo de cada oración, así como algunas de las palabras que forman parte del modismo.

Tercer paso. Practica el uso de los modismos al leer una historia
Cada una de las cortas, pero interesantes historias te permiten comprender cómo se emplean los modismos en situaciones reales. Puedes aumentar tu conocimiento de los modismos e incluso comenzar a sonar como un nativo si practicas la historia y respondes las preguntas.

Preface

Idiom Attack – Everyday Living is a collection of nearly 300 North American idioms in usage today, arranged in a format that is both easy to read and understand, while creating a situational learning format with logical and independently dynamic subject and chapter themes that take the user directly to the subject they want to learn. Arranged in a series of 25 chapters, this text was designed as a learning resource for intermediate to advanced students of English, yet its language was deliberately kept simple enough to also be accessible to high beginners.

An idiom (or phrasal expression) is a set phrase of two or more words that when put together mean something different than the literal meaning of the individual words. As idioms are the idiosyncrasies of a language, they tend to be the most challenging for foreign learners to understand and for teachers to convey. Though complex, they can be indicative of some of the most colorful language used to decorate everyday conversation.

In this text, we've included only the most frequently used, and therefore useful, idioms and phrasal expressions with meanings in both English and Spanish for comparison, examples for a clearer understanding and practical application of the material, and stories for added depth and practice. Literal translations were used for most definitions and sentence translations, yet for some explanations a less literal approach was taken to provide a more natural explanation in the learner's native tongue in order to keep the intention clear. The example sentences provide contextual support for more in-depth understanding of the meanings. The examples have been carefully constructed to support the definition so that in many cases, the meaning may be inferred from the example.

The stories are tailored to be accessible to learners, yet challenge them with the application of language. Following the stories are questions, designed to test the students' comprehension of the story while coaxing them to use the target language.

Finally, additional discussion questions incite deeper dialogue about the subjects raised in the story or in the use of the idioms themselves.

The chapters are organized into 25 areas of interest providing easy access to the target language. Each chapter provides opportunities for reading, writing, listening and speaking. Units can be studied in any order and, by referring to the topic and chapter headings, can provide lessons to supplement other sources.

Idiom Attack may be used as a classroom textbook, as a reference guide, as a supplement for other texts or for self-study. Each chapter can be studied independently of the others so that learners or teachers can easily access the subjects that most need attention. Well suited to the classroom setting or personal study, this book provides an excellent resource for a variety of applications in a user-friendly format.

Idioms are more complex than vocabulary words, but act like them in that they must fit within the grammatical structure of a sentence. Idioms can be used as all parts of speech: noun, verb, adjective or adverb. This book presents idioms in their most common form, but American idioms are a direct reflection of American culture – alive and changing. They are also dynamic in usage. For example, an idiom normally used as a noun may sometimes be used as a verb in a slightly altered form. Such forms, when common, are listed below the idiom definition with an explanation of the altered meaning. A *synonym* following the idiom explanation indicates a similar idiom with the same meaning as above, while an *antonym* indicates the opposite. Useful explanatory notes follow the idiom to explain the complexities of usage or grammar such as hyphenation of the idiom or common inclusion of words of emphasis i.e.- really, just or all. Many idioms also have dual (or more) meanings, which are represented in a cross-reference addendum at the back of the book.

Many idioms may be used interchangeably with different pronouns, such as *I, you, he, she, it, they,* etc. Thus, "one" or "someone" is used in the entry of the idiom to signify such variants. "One" or "one's" is used when the antecedent of the pronoun must refer to the subject of the sentence as in *raise one's voice, cross one's heart* or *mind one's own business.* Similarly, "someone" is used in the idiom when the antecedent of the pronoun must not refer to the grammatical subject of the sentence as in *get in someone's face* or *give someone a start.*

As the entries are arranged non-alphabetically according to each chapter's subject heading, an index is available to easily locate entries alphabetically and an additional list of idioms with dual meanings is cross-referenced for easy comparison.

Thanks for reading and please enjoy the ride. Good luck!

Preface

Ataque de Modismos – La Vida Diaria es una recopilación de 300 modismos norteamericanos que se usan hoy en día, organizados en un formato fácil de leer y comprender conforme a un método de aprendizaje situacional con capítulos lógicos y dinámicos que te llevan directamente al tema que deseas aprender. Este texto, dividido en una serie de 25 capítulos, ha sido diseñado como un recurso de aprendizaje para estudiantes de inglés intermedios y avanzados, pero su lenguaje es lo suficientemente simple como para que también esté al alcance de los principiantes.

Un modismo (o expresión idiomática) es una frase hecha que está compuesta por dos o más palabras que al agruparse tiene un significado diferente que el significado literal de las palabras individuales. Ya que los modismos representan la idiosincrasia de una lengua, es más difícil que su significado sea transmitido por los profesores y comprendido por los estudiantes extranjeros. Aunque son complejos, pueden representar algunos de los lenguajes más coloridos que se emplean para adornar la conversación cotidiana.

En este texto, solo hemos incluido los modismos y expresiones idiomáticas de uso más frecuente con significados tanto en inglés como en español para su comparación, ejemplos para una compresión más clara y aplicación práctica de la materia, e historias para reforzar el conocimiento. La mayoría de definiciones y oraciones fueron traducidas literalmente, pero en otras se adoptó un enfoque menos literal para ofrecer una explicación más natural en la lengua materna del alumno y para mantener clara la intención. Los ejemplos sirven de respaldo contextual para lograr una comprensión más profunda de los significados y han sido construidos cuidadosamente para reforzar la definición. De este modo, en muchos casos, el significado puede deducirse del ejemplo.

Las historias han sido creadas para que sean accesibles a los estudiantes, aunque los desafíen con la aplicación del lenguaje. Luego de estas, aparecen preguntas diseñadas para evaluarlos en la comprensión de la historia mientras que se les persuade a utilizar la lengua meta.

Finalmente, las preguntas adicionales de debate fomentan un diálogo más profundo sobre los temas tratados en la historia o sobre el uso de los mismos modismos.

Los capítulos están organizados en 25 áreas de interés que ofrecen un acceso fácil al idioma meta. Cada capítulo ofrece oportunidades para leer, escribir, escuchar y hablar. Las unidades se pueden estudiar en cualquier orden y, al remitirse a los temas y encabezados de capítulo, pueden ofrecer lecciones para complementar otras fuentes.

Ataque de Modismos puede ser usado como texto de clase, libro de consulta, complemento de otros textos o para el auto-aprendizaje. Cada capítulo puede ser estudiado en forma independiente de modo que los estudiantes o profesores pueden acceder fácilmente a los temas que requieren mayor atención. Muy adecuado para el salón de clases o para estudiar de forma independiente, este libro es un excelente recurso para una variedad de aplicaciones en un formato fácil de usar.

Los modismos son más complejos que las palabras de vocabulario, pero funcionan como ellas en el sentido de que deben encajar dentro de la estructura gramatical de una oración. Los modismos se pueden utilizar como todas las partes de la oración: sustantivo, verbo, adjetivo o adverbio. Este libro presenta los modismos en su forma más común, pero los modismos estadounidenses son el reflejo directo de la cultura estadounidense: vivos y cambiantes. También son dinámicos en su uso. Por ejemplo, un modismo usado normalmente como sustantivo puede ser usado como verbo en una forma ligeramente modificada. Dichas formas, cuando son comunes, aparecen debajo de la definición del modismo con una explicación del significado modificado. Un Sinónimo que aparece luego de la explicación indica un modismo similar y con el mismo significado, mientras que el Antónimo indica lo opuesto. A continuación del modismo, aparecen unas útiles notas que explican las complejidades del uso o la gramática como la separación de sílabas del modismo o la inclusión común de palabras enfáticas p.ej. realmente, solo o todo. Muchos modismos también tienen dos (o más) significados, que están representados en un apéndice de referencias cruzadas en la parte posterior del libro.

Muchos modismos se pueden utilizar indistintamente con pronombres diferentes, como *I, you, he, she, it, they,* etc. Por lo tanto, al inicio del modismo se utiliza uno de ellos o la palabra *someone* para indicar dichas variantes. *One* o *one's* se utiliza cuando el antecedente del pronombre debe referirse al sujeto de la oración como en *raise one's voice* (levantar la voz), *cross one's heart* (prometer), o *mind one's own business* (ocuparse de los asuntos propios). En forma similar, *someone* se utiliza en el modismo cuando el antecedente del pronombre no debe referirse al sujeto gramatical de la oración como en *get in someone's face* (confrontar a alguien) o *give someone a start* (sorprender a alguien).

Ya que las entradas están organizadas de acuerdo al título del capítulo, hay un índice para localizarlas fácilmente en orden alfabético y también una lista adicional de modismos con significados duales para facilitar la comparación.

Gracias por leer y disfruta el viaje. ¡Buena suerte!

How to Use This Book

1 300 modismos esenciales divididos en 25 temas

Los modismos más utilizados, tales como aquellos relacionados con la vida diaria, acciones, emociones, trabajo y negocios, están clasificados en 25 temas. Para cada tema, se presentan entre 10 y 15 modismos junto con ejemplos. A lo largo de este libro, encontrarás más de 300 modismos claves para conversar en inglés.

2 Familiarización de los modismos a través del español

En primer lugar, describimos el significado de los modismos mediante palabras en español y luego te enseñamos cómo se emplean a través de ejemplos en inglés. Este método te permitirá aprender el uso y el significado de los modismos de una manera más fácil y eficaz.

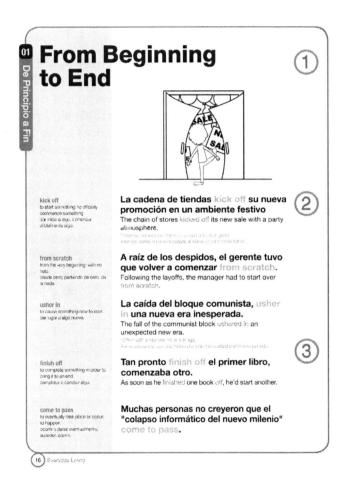

01 De Principio a Fin

From Beginning to End ①

kick off
to start something; to officially commence something
dar inicio a algo; comenzar oficialmente algo.

La cadena de tiendas kick off **su nueva promoción en un ambiente festivo** ②
The chain of stores kicked off its new sale with a party atmosphere.

from scratch
from the very beginning; with no help
desde cero; partiendo de cero, de la nada.

A raíz de los despidos, el gerente tuvo que volver a comenzar from scratch.
Following the layoffs, the manager had to start over from scratch.

usher in
to cause something new to start
dar lugar a algo nuevo.

La caída del bloque comunista, usher in **una nueva era inesperada.**
The fall of the communist block ushered in an unexpected new era.

finish off
to complete something in order to bring it to an end
completar o concluir algo.

Tan pronto finish off **el primer libro, comenzaba otro.** ③
As soon as he finished one book off, he'd start another.

come to pass
to eventually take place or occur; to happen
ocurrir o darse eventualmente; suceder; ocurrir.

Muchas personas no creyeron que el "colapso informático del nuevo milenio" come to pass.

⑯ Everyday Living

3 Aprende cómodamente con explicaciones detalladas

La detallada explicación en inglés del significado del modismo que aparece en la oración de ejemplo transmite los matices de su significado. Además, se define en español. Se incluyen sinónimos, antónimos, notas y explicaciones para facilitar el uso de los modismos en varias maneras.

>> Escucha las grabaciones de los ejemplos y las explicaciones en inglés

(4)

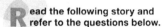

Answers 1. sleepyhead 2. got (himself) going 3. got (up) on the wrong side (of the) bed 4. sleep in 5. morning breath 6. start the (day) off right 7. crack of dawn 8. slept like (a) log 9. (didn't) sleep a wink 10. go off 11. get ready 12. wake up

Read the following story and refer to the questions below.

- Strange Sleepyhead

Let me tell you about my friend Mark, he is quite a funny fellow. Mark is a big sleepyhead. He usually doesn't hear his alarm go off in the morning, so as a result he sleeps in and ends up late for work. Because he sleeps like a log during the night, it is often difficult for him to get himself going in the morning. He never has enough time to get ready and usually forgets to brush his teeth. He has terrible morning breath.

I told him yesterday that I think he should try to get up earlier and start the day off right with some exercise at the crack of dawn, but I think he got up on the wrong side of the bed because he seemed angry at my suggestion.

Anyway, I can't understand him. Yesterday, I couldn't sleep a wink because of all the stress that my boss has been giving me at work. In some ways, I envy Mark and in some ways, I just think that he is strange!

Questions about the story
1. What kind of person is Mark in the morning?
2. Why is he usually late for work?
3. Why is it hard for him to get himself going?
4. Why does Mark have morning breath?
5. What should he do to get himself going?
6. Why does Mark's friend think that he got up on the wrong side of the bed?
7. Why does Mark's friend envy him?

In the Morning (25)

4 Refuerza tu comprensión al llenar los espacios en blanco

Refuerza el significado de los modismos a medida que completas los espacios en blanco de las oraciones de ejemplo. Estas tienen su traducción justo debajo de ellas y contienen una o dos palabras como claves, lo que te permite llenar fácilmente los espacios en blanco y familiarizarte hasta con los modismos más difíciles.

5 Lee las historias para comprender los modismos en contexto

Las cortas e interesantes historias te permiten echar un vistazo a la vida cotidiana de las personas en América del Norte. En cada una de estas se incluye los modismos explicados en el capítulo, lo cual te permite ver cómo se utilizan en varios contextos y cómo hacen más dinámicas las conversaciones.

>> Escucha las grabaciones de las historias

6 Emplea modismos mientras haces y respondes preguntas, y participas en debates

Las preguntas de comprensión y las preguntas para debatir los temas correspondientes al capítulo incluyen modismos que dan a los lectores más oportunidades para utilizarlos activamente al hacer y responder preguntas.

¡Enfréntate al Ataque de Modismos y domina el inglés!

Table of Contents

❶ Everyday Living La vida diaria

Getting Used to Idioms Cómo habituarse a los modismos / **4**

Preface Prólogo / **6**

How to Use This Book Cómo usar este libro / **10**

01. From Beginning to End De Principio a Fin / **16**
kick off / from scratch / usher in / finish off / come to pass / turn over a new leaf / draw to a close /
(not over) until the fat lady sings / start the ball rolling

02. In the Morning En la Mañana / **21**
go off / crack of dawn / wake up / sleep in / morning breath / get ready / start the day off right /
sleep like a log / not sleep a wink / sleepyhead / get up on the wrong side of the bed /
get oneself/someone going

03. In the Evening Por la Noche / **27**
stay up / stay out / stay in / wait up / go out / tired out / fall asleep / go to sleep / after hours /
hit the sack / crash

04. Moments in Time Situaciones en Tiempo / **33**
so far / in no time / at once / as soon as / in the long run / right away / without a doubt / just about to /
at the last minute / not miss a beat / in a heartbeat / all of a sudden / in a flash / in the short term /
in the long term / down the road

05. Weather Conditions Condiciones Climáticas / **39**
cloud up / rain cats and dogs / rain buckets / clear up / heat up / heat wave / come down in sheets /
die down / dry up / cool off / cold spell / killer weather / crazy weather / sticky weather / spitting /
pea soup fog

06. Going to School Yendo a Clases / **47**
hit the books / brush up (on) / cram / pop quiz / sign up / handout / bookworm / hand in / teacher's pet / flunk out / drop out / skip school / ace

07. Gone Shopping Ir de Compras / **53**
window shop / shop around / pick up / be sold out (of) / on sale / snap up / hunt for bargains / pick out / stock up (on) / buy up / take back / rain check

08. Traffic, Travel & Turns Tráfico, Viajes y Giros / **59**
turn around / hang a left/right / up to speed / run a (red) light / as far as / pull over / pull into / make a wrong turn / make a U-turn / bumper-to-bumper / stop and go / gridlock / fender bender

09. Dining Comer / **65**
grab a bite / eat out / leftovers / takeout / junk food / potluck / have a craving for / pig out / wolf down / doggy bag / have a sweet tooth / eat up

10. Housework Quehaceres Domésticos / **71**
take out / clean up / pick up / straighten up / make food / do the dishes / fix up / clean house / odds and ends / garage sale / clean out / spring cleaning / put something back / keep house / upkeep

11. Special Dates & Events Fechas y Eventos Especiales / **78**
hold an event / take place / go off / be rained out / fall through / turn out (for) / turn away / sellout / come up

12. Telephone Talk Conversaciones Telefónicas / **83**
make a call / call (someone) up / on the phone / off the phone / hold on / hang up / get cut off / hang up on someone / off the hook / on the hook / call someone back / make a prank call / over the phone

13. Making Conversation Haciendo Conversación / **90**
make small talk / shoot the breeze / break the ice / strike up a conversation / shake hands / a sight for sore eyes / have not seen someone for ages / have not seen someone in a dog's age / long time no see / what's up / catch you later / see you around / take care

Table of Contents

14. He Said, She Said Él dijo, Ella dijo / **97**
(a) penny for your thoughts / hold it down / fire away / speak one's mind / clam up /
off the top of one's head / blurt out / have a way with words / beat around the bush /
get one's message across / cat got your tongue

15. Fact or Opinion Hecho u Opinión / **102**
for a fact / hear of / know-how / broaden one's horizons / pick up / be news to someone /
through the grapevine / make of / get wind of / in the know / in the loop

16. Human Interaction Interacción Humana / **108**
hit it off (with someone) / got along with / make friends / get in someone's face /
rub elbows with / get together / face to face / tie the knot / on the rocks / break it off /
split up / start off on the wrong foot

17. Family Matters Cosas de Familia / **114**
come from / give birth to / flesh and blood / grow up / bring up / powwow / hand down /
take after / settle down / black sheep / hand-me-down

18. Dating & Relationships Citas y Relaciones / **119**
stand someone up / go out on a date / make out / break up / go steady / knockout / hot /
get dumped / ex-boyfriend / set up / old flame / make up / blind date

19. Visiting Friends Visitando Amigos / **125**
come over / drop in on / show someone in / stopover / swing by / get together / pay a visit /
make someone feel at home / have a seat / visit with / make oneself feel at home / be my guest /
see someone out

20. Social Invitations Invitaciones Sociales / **131**
have someone over / how about / take a rain check / be free / turn down / tag along /
ask someone out / take someone up on something / go along (with) / shoot someone down

21. Relaxing Relajándose / **137**
take it easy / take a nap / daydream / kick back / take a break / lounge around / take a load off /
have free time / kill time / loosen up / pass the time

22. On Holiday De Vacaciones / **143**
on leave / see someone off / have time off / take in / check in / check out (of) / go away / be booked up / wake up call / book something / go sightseeing / get back / take (time) off

23. Sickness Enfermedad / **150**
run a fever / take a turn for the worse / feel out of it / be under the weather / feel/be run down / sick as a dog / catch a cold / feel a cold coming on / going around / be laid up / run its course / get a checkup / get over

24. Trouble & Ease Problemas y Calma / **156**
open (up) a can of worms / be a no-brainer / run into trouble / in a jam / in dire straits / be in over one's head / without a hitch / ups and downs / be up against / be a piece of cake

25. Descriptions & Explanations Descripciones y Explicaciones / **161**
brand new / clear-cut / first-rate / spick and span / out of this world / out of the ordinary / paint a picture / dog-eared / be the pits / up to date

Index Índice / **167**

Crossword Answers Respuestas a los crucigramas / **172**

From Beginning to End

kick off
to start something; to officially commence something.
dar inicio a algo; comenzar oficialmente algo.

La cadena de tiendas kick off **su nueva promoción en un ambiente festivo**
The chain of stores kicked off its new sale with a party atmosphere.
*Informal, as with the first kick to start a football game.
Informal, como la primera patada al iniciar un partido de fútbol.

from scratch
from the very beginning; with no help.
desde cero; partiendo de cero; de la nada.

A raíz de los despidos, el gerente tuvo que volver a comenzar from scratch.
Following the layoffs, the manager had to start over from scratch.

usher in
to cause something new to start.
dar lugar a algo nuevo.

La caída del bloque comunista, usher in **una nueva era inesperada.**
The fall of the communist bloc ushered in an unexpected new era.
*Often with a new period, era or age.
A menudo se usa con una nueva era, una nueva edad o un nuevo periodo.

finish off
to complete something in order to bring it to an end.
completar o concluir algo.

Tan pronto finish off **el primer libro, comenzaba otro.**
As soon as he finished one book off, he'd start another.

come to pass
to eventually take place or occur; to happen.
ocurrir o darse eventualmente; suceder, ocurrir.

Muchas personas no creyeron que el "colapso informático del nuevo milenio" come to pass.

***Synonym** come about.

Many people didn't believe the "Millennium Bug" would come to pass.
*Usually something unplanned.
Usualmente algo no planificado

turn over a new leaf
to make a fresh start; to change course.
empezar una nueva etapa en la vida; realizar un cambio de 180 grados.

He decidido turn over a new leaf **y dejar de fumar.**
I've decided to turn over a new leaf and quit smoking.

draw to a close
come to an end; to finish.
acercarse a su final; estar por terminar.
***Synonym** come to an end.

Mientras el largo verano draw to a close**, nos pusimos a pensar en todo lo que nos divertimos.**
As the long summer drew to a close, we thought back on the fun we had.
*Usually something that happens slowly or 'drawn out'.
Por lo general, algo que ocurre lentamente o algo que esta por acabarse.

(not over) until the fat lady sings
something is not over until it's completely over; there's still a chance to win or there is still time remaining.
nada está dicho hasta no acabar y llegar al final; aún hay posibilidades de ganar o aún hay tiempo.

Oye, no te vayas aún. No se acaba until the fat lady sings.
Hey, don't leave yet. It's not over until the fat lady sings.

start the ball rolling
to get something underway; to start something and keep the momentum from dying or dwindling down; to begin.
poner algo en marcha; empezar algo y evitar que desaparezca; empezar.
***Synonym** get the ball rolling.

Kelly los guiará a todos en una canción para start the ball rolling.
Kelly will lead you all in a song to start the ball rolling.

Fill in the blanks with the appropriate idioms.

01 Sadly, the relationship between the children _____ to a _____ and they eventually forgot about each other.

Lamentablemente, la relación entre los niños llegó a su fin y terminaron olvidándose el uno del otro.

02 The invention of the automobile _____ _____ the era of the horseless carriage.

El invento de los automóviles dio lugar a la era del carruaje sin caballo.

03 The weeklong festival known as All Saint's Day _____ off this Sunday.

El festival con duración de una semana que se inicia este domingo, es conocido como Día de Todos los Santos.

04 Mr. MacDonald started _____ _____ three times before finally becoming successful.

El Sr. MacDonald comenzó tres veces desde cero antes de alcanzar finalmente el éxito.

05 It's hard for a drug addict to _____ _____ a new _____ and stop substance abuse.

Es muy difícil para un drogadicto realizar un cambio de 180 grados y frenar el abuso de sustancias.

06 If you don't get started, you'll never be able to finish and go home. Why don't you just _____ the ball _____?

Si no te pones a trabajar, no vas a terminar y regresar a casa. Sugiero que te pongas en marcha.

07 The children were never able to _____ _____ an entire ice cream sundae, but they had fun trying.

Los niños no fueron capaces de terminar todo el helado, perose divirtieron intentándolo.

08 People say that bad luck comes in threes. I've had two bad things happen to me and I hope that the third never _____ to _____.

La gente dice que la mala suerte viene de a tres, ya me han pasado dos cosas malas y espero que la tercera nunca ocurra.

09 We may be losing the game, but don't count us out yet. It's not over _____ the _____ _____ _____.

Es probable que estemos perdiendo el juego, pero no nos den por vencidos. Nada está dicho hasta no llegar al final.

Answers 1. drew (to a) close 2. ushered in 3. kicks (off) 4. from scratch 5. turn over (a new) leaf 6. start (the ball) rolling 7. finish off 8. comes (to) pass 9. (not over) until (the) fat lady sings

R ead the following story and refer to the questions below.

- Shaping Minds

Though our class was drawing to a close, we looked back on the experiences of the last year and realized what had come to pass was something special. Our teacher had hoped that with his help we could turn over a new leaf. He helped to usher in a new era for us as we went off to college or work, changing from children to adults.

He had started the ball rolling for us, but it was the change in him that was the greatest. As we finished off the year getting ready to leave, we thought of how our year had kicked off and how unkind we had been to him. Each of us had changed and so had he, as he learned to be patient with us.

I suppose each year he has to start from scratch to build his students up, getting them ready for the future. Though we realized that everything must end at some point, we didn't want the fat lady to sing until we had a chance to say our goodbyes and give our thanks. So here's to you, for all you did and all you gave to us. Thank you!

Questions about the story

1. As the year drew to a close, what did the students realize?
2. What did the teacher hope to help the students do?
3. What had been his main goal? Did he reach it?
4. As the year kicked off, what did he do?
   What did the students do?
5. Through helping the students, how had he helped himself?
6. Why did he have to start from scratch?
7. What didn't they want to happen?

Questions for discussion

1. How do you feel when the school year draws to a close?

2. When you meet someone new, how do you start the ball rolling?

3. How would you like to kick off the New Year next year?

4. What things are better when started from scratch?

5. Have you ever tried to turn over a new leaf?
Describe the situation.

The end

Dando forma a la mente

Aunque nuestra clase estaba llegando a su fin, repasamos nuestras experiencias del año pasado y nos dimos cuenta de que lo que sucedió fue algo especial. Nuestro profesor esperó que con su ayuda pudiéramos hacer un cambio de 180 grados. Nos ayudó a dar inicio a una nueva era mientras nos encaminábamos a estudiar o trabajar, pasando de niños a adultos.

El ya había comenzado a ponernos en marcha, pero lo más grandioso fue el cambio en él. Mientras terminábamos el año y nos preparábamos para irnos pensamos en como comenzó nuestro año y la manera poco amable en que lo tratamos. Cada uno de nosotros había cambiado y también el, ya que aprendió a ser paciente con nosotros.

Supongo que cada año tiene que comenzar desde cero para instruir a sus estudiantes, preparándolos para el futuro. Si bien nos dimos cuenta de que todo inicio tiene su fin, no quisimos dar las cosas por terminadas hasta haber tenido la oportunidad de despedirnos y dar nuestras gracias. Así que esto es para usted por todo lo que ha hecho y nos ha dado. ¡Muchas gracias!

In the Morning

go off
to make a noise; for an alarm to ring or sound.
hacer un ruido; cuando una alarma hace ruido o suena.

Jason no escuchó la alarma go off por la mañana y llegó tarde a su entrevista de trabajo.

Jason didn't hear his alarm go off in the morning and he ended up late for his job interview.

crack of dawn
daybreak; the moment when sunlight is first seen in the morning sky.
amanecer; el momento en que se ve por primera vez la luz del sol en el cielo.

Nos vamos a levantar al crack of dawn para ir a esquiar mañana.

We are going to get up at the crack of dawn to go skiing tomorrow.

wake up
to rouse from sleep; to stir and open one's eyes in the morning.
despertar de un sueño; acción de abrir los ojos por la mañana.
Synonym get up.

Cuando era joven me wake up temprano por la mañana, pero ahora me wake up más tarde.

When I was young I woke up early in the morning, but now I wake up much later.

*Some people 'wake up' and 'get up' at the same time while others 'wake up', stay in bed and then 'get up' later.
Algunas personas se 'despiertan' y 'levantan' a la misma vez, mientras que otras se 'despiertan', permanecen en cama y se levantan después.

sleep in
to sleep later than normal.
quedarse dormido; dormir hasta tarde.

El día de mañana que es su día libre, Erica va a sleep in pues trabajó muy duro durante toda la semana.

Erica is going to sleep in on her day off tomorrow because she worked hard all week long.

morning breath
bad breath in the morning.
mal aliento por la mañana.

¡Don tiene morning breath! No aguanto conversar con él por la mañana.

Don has terrible morning breath! I can't stand talking to him in the morning.

* This idiom is usually used for someone very close.
Esta expresión generalmente se utiliza con personas de confianza.

get ready
to prepare oneself.
alistarse, prepararse.

Me toma más o menos cuarenta y cinco minutos get ready por las mañanas.

It takes me about forty-five minutes to get ready in the morning.

* Usually used for the day ahead, which would include washing, getting dressed and eating.
Usualmente utilizado como expresión para el día siguiente, incluye el tiempo que uno toma en lavarse, vestirse y comer.

start the day off right
to begin the day with something good or something that feels right.
iniciar el día con algo bueno o algo que haga que uno se sienta bien.

Por la mañana, Tom ordena su escritorio para start the day off right.

Tom cleans his desk up at work in the morning to start the day off right.

* Habitual behavior that one feels strange without in the morning.
Comportamiento habitual por la mañana sin el cual uno se siente incómodo.

sleep like a log
to sleep deeply; to sleep soundly.
dormir profundamente; dormir bien.
* **Synonym** sleep like a baby.

Estoy muy cansado. Es muy probable que sleep like a log hoy noche.

I'm really tired. I will probably sleep like a log tonight.

not sleep a wink
to get very little or no sleep at all.
dormir muy poco o no dormir en lo absoluto.

La niña Emma estaba tan emocionada la noche antes de Navidad que not sleep a wink.

Little Emma was so excited the night before Christmas that she didn't sleep a wink.

sleepyhead
someone who continues to feel sleepy or drowsy after waking up.
alguien que continúa con sueño o somnolencia después de haberse despertado. España: dormilón.

Me siento un sleepyhead esta mañana. He tomado dos tazas de café pero aún no puedo despertarme.

I feel like such a sleepyhead this morning. I have had 2 cups of coffee, but I still can't seem to wake up.

*An expression that indicates one's mental state is not fully awake or coherent. Expresion que indica que el estado mental de uno no esta del todo despierto o coherente.)

get up on the wrong side of the bed

to be upset or in a bad mood from the moment one gets up.
estar molesto o de mal humor desde que uno se despierta; levantarse con el pie izquierdo.

Pienso que hoy día me get up on the wrong side of the bed**. He estado de mal humor toda la mañana.**

I think that I got up on the wrong side of the bed today. I have been in a bad mood all morning.

*Usually used to refer to someone in a bad mood.
Por lo general se utiliza para referirse a alguien que se encuentra de mal humor.

get oneself/ someone going

to stimulate someone in the morning, causing them to have a feeling of being awake.
estimular a alguien por la mañana, haciendo que se sientan más despiertos y energéticos; empezar a funcionar.

Una taza de café y un poco de ejercicio realmente me get me going **por las mañanas.**

A cup of coffee and a little exercise really get me going in the morning.

F ill in the blanks with the appropriate idioms.

01 I can't seem to wake up this morning. I feel like such a _____.
Parece que no me puedo despertar esta mañana. Me siento soñoliento.

02 Mark often jumps rope in the morning to _____ himself _____.
Mark a menudo salta cuerda por la mañana para ponerse en marcha.

03 Something must be wrong with the boss today. I think that he _____ up on _____ _____ _____ of the _____ this morning.
Algo le sucede hoy al jefe. Creo que se levantó con el pie izquierdo esta mañana.

04 I think that I am just going to relax and _____ _____ this Sunday.
Pienso que este domingo voy a relajarme y quedarme en cama

05 OOOH WEE! Did you talk to Ralph? He has a bad case of _____ _____. I wouldn't stand too close to him to talk if I were you.
¡Uyuyuy! ¿Hablaste con Ralph? Tiene un terrible problema de mal aliento por la mañana. De ser tú no me acercaría mucho para hablar con él.

06 I like to _____ _____ day _____ _____ by reading the newspaper and meditating in the morning before I head off to work.
Me gusta empezar bien el día leyendo el periódico y meditando por las mañanas antes de dirigirmo al trabajo.

07 Our coach made the whole team get up at the _____ _____ _____ to start practice today. I think that there must be something wrong with him.
El día de hoy, nuestro entrenador hizo que todo el equipo se levantara al amanecer. Pienso que anda mal de la cabeza.

08 You _____ _____ a _____ for twelve hours. You must have been really tired.
Dormiste como un tronco por doce horas. De seguro estabas muy cansado.

09 I was so excited about the new trip that I didn't _____ _____ _____ the night before I left.
Estaba tan entusiasmado por el nuevo viaje que no pegué el ojo la noche anterior al viaje.

10 I am sorry that I am late. I didn't hear my alarm _____ _____.
Siento mucho llegar tarde. No escuché la alarma sonar.

11 How long will it take you to _____ _____ for school?
¿Cuánto tiempo te toma prepararte para la escuela?

12 What time do you usually _____ _____ in the morning?
Usualmente, ¿a qué hora te levantas por las mañanas?

Read the following story and refer to the questions below.

- Strange Sleepyhead

Let me tell you about my friend Mark. He is quite a funny fellow! Mark is a big sleepyhead. He usually doesn't hear his alarm go off in the morning, so as a result he sleeps in and ends up late for work. Because he sleeps like a log during the night, it is often difficult for him to get himself going in the morning. He never has enough time to get ready and usually forgets to brush his teeth. He has terrible morning breath!

I told him yesterday that I think he should try to get up earlier and start the day off right with some exercise at the crack of dawn, but I think he got up on the wrong side of the bed because he seemed angry at my suggestion.

Anyway, I can't understand him. Yesterday, I couldn't sleep a wink because of all the stress that my boss has been giving me at work. In some ways, I envy Mark, and in some ways I just think that he is strange!

Questions about the story

1. What kind of person is Mark in the morning?
2. Why is he usually late for work?
3. Why is it hard for him to get himself going?
4. Why does Mark have morning breath?
5. What should he do to get himself going?
6. Why does Mark's friend think that he got up on the wrong side of the bed?
7. Why does Mark's friend envy him?

Questions for discussion

1. Do you usually get up right when you wake up in the morning?

2. Are you a sleepyhead in the morning?

3. Do you do anything to start the day off right? What?

4. Do you ever wake up at the crack of dawn?

5. How do you usually get yourself going in the morning?

6. How long does it take for you to get ready in the morning?

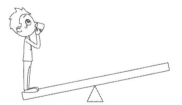

Extraño dormilón

Permítanme contarles sobre mi amigo Mark, él es un tipo bastante gracioso. Mark es un dormilón. Generalmente no escucha el sonido de su alarma por la mañana, entonces se queda dormido y llega tarde al trabajo. Debido a que duerme como un tronco por la noche, a menudo se le hace difícil ponerse en marcha por la mañana. Nunca tiene suficiente tiempo para prepararse y a menudo se olvida cepillarse los dientes. Tiene mal aliento por la mañana. Ayer le dije que debería levantarse mas temprano y empezar bien el dia haciendo ejercicios al amanecer, pero creo que se levanto con el pie izquierdo porque se mostró muy enfadado con mi sugerencia.

Como fuese, no lo entiendo. Ayer, no pude pegar el ojo debido a todo el estrés que mi jefe me ha estado causando en el trabajo. En cierto modo, envidio a Mark y en cierto modo pienso que es extraño.

In the Evening

03

Por la Noche

stay up
to not go to bed at the normal time;
to pass the night without sleep.
no ir a dormir a la hora normal;
quedarse despierto toda la noche.

Entre semana usualmente me stay up **hasta las once en punto y luego me voy a acostar.**
On weekdays, I usually stay up until eleven o'clock, and then I go to bed.
*Often followed by 'until' with a specific time indicated afterwards.
Por lo general seguido por 'until' con un tiempo especifico en futuro.

stay out
to be away from home in the evening or at night.
no estar en casa en la noche.

Hanna obtuvo permiso de sus padres para stay out **pasado la media noche.**
Hannah had permission from her parents to stay out past midnight.
*Usually, a specific time is indicated to note the return home. If no time is mentioned the activity is usually indefinite.
Por lo general seguido por 'until' con un tiempo especifico en futuro.

stay in
to be at home during the evening.
quedarse en casa durante la noche.
*__Antonym__ stay out.

Rick tuvo que stay in **y estudiar porque tenía prueba en su escuela al siguiente día.**
Rick had to stay in and study because he had a test the next day at school.

wait up
to remain awake while waiting for a person to return home;
to remain awake while waiting for an event to happen.

Pienso que Judy se preocupa demasiado, ella wait up **a su hijo sin acostarse cada noche que él sale.**
I think that Judy worries too much, because she waits

permanecer despierto mientras se espera el retorno a casa de alguna persona; permanecer despierto mientras se espera el inicio de algún evento.

go out
to socialize away from home or experience a recreational activity out of the house.
socializar fuera de casa o experimentar una actividad de recreación fuera de casa.

tired out
exhausted or having no energy remaining; thoroughly tired.
estar agotado o no tener energías; sentir profundo cansancio.

fall asleep
to go to sleep; to begin sleeping.
ir a dormir; comenzar a dormir.
Synonym nod off; doze off.

go to sleep
to begin sleeping; to lie down to sleep.
ir a dormir; acostarse en cama y dormir.
Synonym turn in; go to bed.

after hours
after normal business or school hours or after a permitted time; late at night.
después de horas de escuela o trabajo, o después de la hora permitida; tarde por la noche.

up every night her son goes out.
*This idiom is most often used when parents remain awake until their children arrive at home.
Este modismo se suele utilizar cuando los padres de familia se quedan despiertos hasta que sus hijos regresen a casa.

Antes de casarme solía go out tres veces a la semana.
Before I got married, I used to go out about three times a week.
*This idiom is generally used in the evening.
Este modismo se suele utilizar en la noche.

Tom se fue a dormir temprano porque estaba tired out como para permanecer despierto.
Tom went to sleep early because he felt too tired out to stay up.

John se acuesta a las once en punto pero no fall asleep sino hasta las doce.
John goes to bed at eleven o'clock, but doesn't fall asleep until twelve.
*This idiom refers to the moment when one loses consciousness.
Este modismo hace referencia al momento en que uno pierde la conciencia.

Nancy tiene que trabajar temprano entre semana por eso go to sleep todas las noches a las 10:30.
Nancy needs to work early on weekdays, so she goes to sleep at 10:30 every night.

El dueño del club nocturno no puede servir tragos after hours.
The nightclub owner cannot serve alcohol after hours.
*This idiom is most commonly used when speaking about bars and dance clubs.
Este modismo se utiliza con mayor frecuencia cuando se habla de bares y centros nocturnos.
**This idiom is generally used to express that something is happening after a normal or designated time. For example, a bar that is open after normal operating hours is an 'after hours bar' and a later than normal nighttime visit is called an 'after hours visit'.

hit the sack
to go to bed to sleep; to retire for the night.
ir a cama para dormir; cesar actividades por la noche.
*_Synonym_ hit the hay.

Katie no aguantaba estar despierta así que hit the sack después de que sus amigos se fueron.

Katie could not keep her eyes open, so she hit the sack after her friends had left.

crash
to fall asleep from exhaustion.
quedarse dormido debido al cansancio.
*_Synonym_ crash out.

Tan pronto Mark llega a casa después del trabajo se crash por una hora antes de la cena.

As soon as Mark gets home from work, he crashes for an hour before dinner.

*'Crash out' may be used when sleeping at someone's house for free.
'Crash out' puede ser utilizado cuando uno duerme gratis en la casa de otra persona.

F ill in the blanks with the appropriate idioms.

01 Pauline was too tired to stay up with her friends, so she decided to _____ to _____ early.

Pauline estaba demasiado cansada como para trasnochar con sus amigos, así que decidió ir a dormir temprano.

02 The dance club was more fun than they had expected, so Samantha and Veronica chose to _____ _____ for another hour.

El club estuvo más divertido que lo esperado por eso Samantha y Verónica decidieron quedarse una hora más.

03 The students made plans to study for two hours, then _____ _____ afterwards to have some fun.

Los estudiantes planificaron estudiar por dos horas para después salir a divertirse.

04 As soon as her tired baby brother was in the car seat and they started moving, Jennifer knew he would _____ _____ quickly.

Inmediatamente después de que su cansado hermanito fue colocado en el asiento del carro y comenzaron a conducir, Jennifer supo que se quedaría dormido inmediatamente.

05 On the day before the big race, Alex did not want to be_____ _____, so he ran slower than usual.

El día anterior a la gran carrera, Alex no quiso agotarse así que corrió mas lento que lo usual.

06 The children knew that since it was a school night, they would not be allowed to _____ _____ late.

Los niños sabían que por ser noche de clases, no los iban a dejar trasnochar.

07 No alcohol was permitted at the new _____-_____ club.

No se permitía alcohol en el nuevo club después de horas.

08 When Johan's mother worries, she_____ up for him until he returns home.

Cuando la mamá de Johan se preocupa, espera sin dormir hasta que él retorne a casa.

09 "I am too tired to go to a third nightclub. I need to _____ soon."

"Estoy demasiado cansado como para ir a un tercer club nocturno, necesito ir a dormir pronto."

10 Soon after the clock struck nine, Dan looked to his son and said, "It's time for you to hit _____ _____."

Inmediatamente después de que el reloj dio las 9, Dan miró a su hijo y le dijo, "Es hora de que vayas a dormir."

11 Rather than go out partying this Saturday, let's just _____ _____ and watch movies.

En vez de salir a bailar este sábado, simplemente quedémonos en casa y veamos películas.

Read the following story and refer to the questions below.

- Late night lesson

Johan was planning to go out to see the new Jackie Chan movie on Friday evening. He asked permission to stay out with his friends past midnight. Johan's mother told him that he could go out, but that he should not stay up too late the night before. If he did not go to bed early on Thursday evening, he would be too tired out on Friday. Johan agreed with his mother and decided to turn in. He hit the sack early thinking he'd be sound asleep before ten o'clock.

Johan was excited to go out to the after hours club on Friday following the movie. He tried to fall asleep, but the thought of next evening's events kept him awake.

On Friday night, Johan stayed out until dawn and when he came home, his mother was waiting up for him. His mother tried to discipline him, but Johan was too tired to listen and just went to his bedroom to crash.

Questions about the story

1. What was Johan planning to do on Friday evening?
2. What did he ask his mother for?
3. Why did his mother say that he should not stay up too late the night before?
4. Where did Johan go after he saw the movie on Friday night?
5. What time did he stay out until?
6. What was his mother doing when Johan finally came home?
7. Did Johan's mother discipline Johan? Why or why not?

Questions for discussion

1. What was the latest that you have ever stayed up?
When was it and why did you do it?

2. Where in your city can someone go after hours to drink or dance?

3. What time do you usually turn in at night?

4. Do (or Did) your parents ever wait up for you?

5. How often do you go out each week?

6. Will you wait up for your children when they are older and going out? Why?

Lección nocturna

Johan planeaba salir el viernes por la noche a ver la nueva película de Jackie Chan. Pidió permiso para quedarse con sus amigos pasada la media noche. Su mamá le dio permiso para salir, pero le dijo que no debía trasnochar la noche anterior a su salida. Si no se iba a dormir temprano el jueves por la noche, iba a estar demasiado agotado el viernes. Johan se puso de acuerdo con su madre y cedió. Se fue a dormir temprano pensando que se quedaría profundamente dormido antes de las 10 de la noche.

Johan estaba emocionado por el hecho de que iba a salir a un club nocturno el día viernes después de la película. Intento quedarse dormido, pero el solo pensar en lo que ocurriría al próximo día lo mantuvo despierto. El viernes por la noche, Johan estuvo fuera de casa hasta el amanecer y cuando regreso a casa, su madre lo estuvo esperando despierta. Su madre trató de disciplinarlo pero Johan estaba demasiado cansado y se dirigio a su cama para dormir.

Moments in Time

so far
as of yet; up to this point or to a limited extent.
hasta el momento; hasta un punto descrito o hasta un tiempo límite.
*__Synonym__ so far, so good.

So far donde sé, tiene una carrera prometedora en Samsung.
So far as I know, he has a promising career with Samsung.

in no time
in a relatively short time; within a very short period of time; almost instantly.
en un plazo relativamente corto; dentro de poco tiempo; casi inmediatamente.
*__Synonym__ in a jiffy.

Está bien Jefe, haré el trabajo in no time.
OK boss, I'll get the job done in no time.

at once
at the same time; immediately.
al mismo tiempo; inmediatamente.

Como podía hacer varias cosas at once, logró terminar la universidad mientras trabajaba en dos lugares.
Since he could do several things at once, he managed to finish university while keeping two jobs.

as soon as
right away at the end of one thing; immediately starting something else.
inmediatamente después de un hecho; seguido de algo; en cuanto.
*__Synonym__ ASAP.

as soon as abrió la tienda, la gente entró tumultuosamente para obtener los descuentos.
As soon as the store opened, the people came rushing in for the sale.

*This idiom is usually followed by 'possible' or 'I can.'
Este modismo usualmente viene seguido de 'possible' o 'I can'

in the long run
over a lengthy period of time; eventually; at some point in time in the future.
en un periodo de tiempo largo; eventualmente; en un momento en futuro.

Estudiar dedicadamente todos los días me hará mas exitoso in the long run.

Studying hard every day will make me more successful in the long run.

right away
without delay; immediately.
sin retraso; inmediatamente.

Mi mamá dijo que tengo que ordenar mi dormitorio right away**, así que no puedo jugar ahora.**

My mom said I have to clean my room right away, so I can't play now.

without a doubt
without question; certainly; definitely.
sin lugar a duda; en honor a la verdad; definitivamente.

without a doubt **puedes contar conmigo para tu boda.**

Without a doubt, you can count on me to be at your wedding.

just about to
intend to do something; intend to start despite some interruption.
tener intención de hacer algo; tener intención de empezar a realizar algo sin importar las interrupciones.

Estaba just about to **hacer mis tareas cuando timbró el teléfono.**

I was just about to do my homework when the phone rang.

*Usually followed by the root form of a verb.
Usualmente seguido por un verbo base.

at the last minute
just before a deadline; with little time remaining before a significant or concluding moment.
justo antes del tiempo de entrega; con muy poco tiempo restante antes de entregar algo de importancia o concluir algo.

Meg tiene el mal hábito de dejar cosas at the last minute **y siempre atrasarse.**

Meg has a habit of starting things at the last minute and always being late.

not miss a beat
without hesitation; continuously or reliably.
sin pensarlo dos veces; continuamente o progresivamente.
Synonym without missing a beat.

El capitán del equipo es tan guapo que puede cambiar de chicas not miss a beat.

The team captain is so handsome that he can go from girlfriend to girlfriend and not miss a beat.

in a heartbeat
in a short period of time; in an instant.
en un plazo de tiempo corto; en un instante.

En Las Vegas tu suerte puede cambiar in a heartbeat.

In Vegas, your luck can change in a heartbeat.

all of a sudden
something happening without warning or in an instant; suddenly.
una situación que pasa inesperadamente sin aviso o al instante; de repente.

Estaba caminando por la calle cuando, all of a sudden Mary apareció.

I was walking down the street when, all of a sudden, Mary appeared.

in a flash
within a very short period of time; instantly.
en un plazo corto de tiempo; instantáneamente.

El dinero que ahorramos en el verano desapareció in a flash cuando comenzó la escuela.

The money we saved over the summer was gone in a flash once school started.

*In this idiom, 'flash' indicates the time it takes for the flash of a camera.
En este modismo, 'flash' indica tiempo comparándolo al flash de una cámara.

in the short term
over a short period of time; involving or lasting a relatively brief amount of time.
en un periodo corto de tiempo; que se refiere o que dura un tiempo breve.

Vivir solo in the short term ha convertido a Harry en una persona egoísta.

Living only in the short term has made Harry into a selfish person.

in the long term
over a lengthy period of time; involving or lasting a relatively lengthy amount of time.
a largo plazo; demorándose o durando un largo tiempo.

Calvin dijo que in the long term él sabe qué actividad traerá mejores recuerdos.

Calvin said that in the long term, he knows which activity will make better memories.

down the road
at some point in the future; in the distance; someday.
en algún momento en el futuro; a la larga; algún día.

No sabemos qué pasará down the road, por eso tenemos que estar preparados.

We never know what's down the road, so we must be prepared for anything.

F ill in the blanks with the appropriate idioms.

01 I understand completely. It won't be late again. This time I'll get it done without _____ _____ .

Lo entiendo claramente. No llegaré tarde de nuevo. Sin lugar a duda, esta vez lo voy a lograr.

02 If he had known what was _____ _____ _____ happen, he never would have left home.

Si hubiese sabido lo que estaba a punto de pasar, nunca habría salido de casa.

03 When I said to do it _____ _____ , I meant today, not when you feel like it.

Cuando dije que lo hicieras inmediatamente, me refería a hoy día, no cuando te de la gana.

04 He went out and was back _____ _____ _____ so we never missed him.

Salió y regresó instantáneamente, así que nunca lo extrañamos.

05 I know all these troubles will make me stronger _____ _____ _____ _____ .

Sé que todos estos problemas me harán más fuerte a largo plazo.

06 The sea was calm when, all _____ _____ _____ , a storm hit us.

El mar estaba tranquilo, cuando de repente cayó la tormenta.

07 I managed my affairs _____ _____ as I could, and then got help for the rest.

Me encargué de mis asuntos lo más que pude y luego obtuve ayuda de otros.

08 Don't worry about the swelling. It will go down _____ _____ _____ .

No te preocupes por la hinchazón. Disminuirá rápidamente.

09 I realize the assignment is late, but just wait and I'll get it done _____ _____ _____ possible.

Reconozco que el trabajo está demorado pero espéreme y lo acabaré tan pronto sea posible.

10 She couldn't understand how he could do several jobs _____ _____ and still have time for his family.

Ella no entendía como él podía trabajar en varios lugares al mismo tiempo y aun así tener tiempo para su familia.

11 Luckily, _____ _____ last _____ a friend came to help Jerry out of his predicament.

Afortunadamente, a último minuto, un amigo de Jerry lo vino a ayudar con el problema.

12 _____ _____ _____ all the struggles of an advanced education will pay off.

En un futuro, todos los sacrificios por obtener educación superior se verán recompensados.

13 A Stanford education will make your goals easy to accomplish in _____

_____ _____ .

A largo plazo, una educación en Stanford te facilitará alcanzar metas.

14 While sitting at home and relaxing has benefits in _____ _____

_____, they don't outweigh the long-term benefits of exercise.

Mientras que sentarse en casa y descansar tiene sus beneficios a un corto plazo, no son más importantes que los beneficios a plazo largo recibidos con el ejercicio.

15 I'll be back to pick you up in _____ _____ , baby, so be ready at the door.

Ya regreso a recogerte inmediatamente, espérame en la puerta.

16 He was so talented that he was able to go from student to professional and _____ _____ _____ beat.

Tenía tanto talento que era capaz de pasar de estudiante a profesional sin vacilar.

Read the following story and refer to the questions below.

- In the Nick of Time

Peter and his wife, Wendy, were just about to leave for Las Vegas on their honeymoon when, all of a sudden, he realized that he had one last thing to do. "I'll be back in a flash," he said as he went into the house.

"You're always doing things at the last minute," Wendy responded, but she knew they would be happier in the long term if she just waited.

He had forgotten to send in a project for work and had to get it done at once. As soon as he got to his computer, he found the file and, in no time, had downloaded it to a disk. "So far, so good," he thought, but then he still had to get it to work and, without a doubt, Wendy would be upset.

He came out of the house saying, "If we go right away, we can drop it off at work and, without missing a beat, be on our way to the airport in a heartbeat." "Sure, honey," she said, thinking that instead of being nervous and upset in the short term, it would be better to be supportive. In the long run, they had a great life ahead of them and down the road none of this would matter.

Questions about the story

1. Where are Peter and his wife going?

2. Why did he go back into the house?

3. What was he doing on the computer?

4. What two things did Peter do in the house?

5. What was the second thing he had to do on the way to the airport?

6. Where were they going on their honeymoon?

7. What did Wendy think about when they left the house?

Questions for discussion

1. Have you ever been late for or missed an airplane? Describe the situation.

2. What are popular honeymoon destinations in your country?

3. What would you do if your wife or husband were working during your vacation?

4. Have you ever forgotten to do something important for work? How did you deal with it?

5. Have you ever had to be supportive of someone even when you were upset with them?

Momento oportuno

Peter y su esposa Wendy estaban a punto de dirigirse a Las Vegas para celebrar su luna de miel, cuando de repente, él se dio cuenta de que tenía una cosa más que hacer. "¡Regresaré inmediatamente!" dijo, mientras se dirigía a la casa. "Siempre dejas todo al último minuto." Wendy respondió, pero ella sabía que estarían más felices a largo plazo si solamente esperaba.

El se había olvidado de enviar un proyecto al trabajo y tenía que hacerlo inmediatamente. Tan pronto llegó a su computadora encontró el archivo, y rápidamente bajó la información a un disco. "Por ahora, todo bien" pensó, pero aún le faltaba hacer que el programa funcione y sin lugar a duda Wendy se enojaría.

Salió de la casa diciendo, "si nos vamos inmediatamente podemos pasar dejándolo por el trabajo y con la misma viada dirigirnos al aeropuerto rápidamente." "Seguro que sí, corazón", dijo ella, mientras pensaba que en vez de estar nerviosa o enojada en ese momento, era mejor apoyarlo. A la larga tenían una vida increíble por delante y en el futuro nada de esto tendría mucha importancia.

Weather Conditions

cloud up
for the sky to become cloudy; to become grey and overcast.
cubrirse de muchas nubes el cielo; oscurecerse y nublarse.

Cuando el cielo se cloud up **me gusta quedarme en casa para leer o hacer deberes.**
When the sky clouds up, I like to stay inside to do housework or read.

rain cats and dogs
to rain hard; to pour with rain.
llover a cántaros; llover densamente. España: caer chuzos de punta.

Mi papá entró a casa empapado y dijo que estaba lloviendo rain cats and dogs.
My dad came into the house dripping wet and said that it was raining cats and dogs outside.

rain buckets
to rain very heavily, all at once; to downpour.
llover pesada y súbitamente; llover torrencialmente.

Candice decidió orillarse en la carretera mientras conducía porque estaba rain buckets.
Candice decided to pull over on the road while driving because it was raining buckets.

clear up
for the sky to become clearer; for bad weather to go away, changing into a better condition.
despejarse el cielo; acabarse el mal clima; pasar a una mejor condición climática.

James se alegró al ver que el clima se clear up **porque solo tenía un día libre para salir de picnic.**
James was happy to see the weather clear up because he had only one day off to go on a picnic.

heat up
for the temperature to rise;
to become warmer.
incrementarse la temperatura;
tornarse más cálido el clima.

En esta parte del país las temperaturas por lo general heat up en junio.
In this part of the country, temperatures usually heat up around June.

heat wave
a period of time during which the weather is much hotter than usual.
periodo de tiempo durante el cual el clima es más caliente que lo usual.

Durante la heat wave mis padres abrieron todas las ventanas y las puertas porque no tenemos aire acondicionado.
During the heat wave, my parents opened all the windows and the doors because we don't have air conditioning.

come down in sheets
to rain very heavily.
llover a cántaros.

Frank se dio cuenta de que su paraguas era inservible ya que estaba come down in sheets y se estaba empapado.
Frank decided that his umbrella was useless since the rain was coming down in sheets and he was soaking wet.

This idiom describes the way rain blown by the wind during a storm can look like sheets of rain in the air.
Este modismo describe la lluvia cuando es empujada por el viento durante una tormenta; este hecho luce como cortinas de lluvia en el aire.

die down
to lose strength; to lessen in power; to weaken.
perder fuerza; debilitarse.
Synonym let up.

Después de que este clima die down voy a revisar mi carro para asegurarme de que esté bien.
After this weather dies down, I am going to go check and see if my car is OK.

dry up
for moisture to evaporate;
to run dry; to make a river, pool or puddle lose all its water.
evaporarse la humedad; dejar de fluir; hacer que un río, piscina o charco se seque.

Cuando el río se dry up en el verano, muchos niños juegan en los charcos y buscan sus juguetes perdidos.
When the river dries up in the summer, many children play on the riverbed and look for lost toys.

cool off
for the temperature to lower;
to become comfortably cool.
bajar la temperatura; enfriar a temperaturas agradables.
Synonym cool down.

Al ponerse el sol la casa usualmente se cool off unos cuantos grados.
When the sun goes down, the house usually cools off a few degrees.

cold spell
a period of extreme cold;
a sudden change from warm
weather to cold.
periodo de frío extremo; cambio repentino
de un clima cálido a un clima frío.
*Synonym cold snap.

killer weather
ruthless or extreme weather.
clima despiadado y fuerte.

crazy weather
extremely abnormal weather.
clima extremadamente inusual.

sticky weather
uncomfortably humid or muggy
weather.
clima húmedo e incómodo.

spitting
to rain very slightly; to rain
scattered droplets of water, usually
just before a rain shower begins.
caer poca lluvia; chispear; caer gotas de
lluvia, usualmente antes que comience
a llover.

pea soup fog
very thick, dense fog.
neblina densa, muy espesa.

Las cañerías de agua de mi casa se congelaron durante la cold spell.

The water pipes in my house froze during the cold spell last year.

Debido al killer weather decidí quedarme adentro.

Because of the killer weather, I decided to stay indoors.

Durante el crazy weather que tuvimos la semana pasada mucha gente perdió sus casas debido a inundaciones, incendios y huracanes.

During the crazy weather we had last week, many people lost their homes due to floods, fires, and hurricanes.

Jenny dijo que se va a poner su vestido más ligero debido al sticky weather del día de hoy.

Jenny said that she is going to wear her lightest dress to school because of the sticky weather today.

Debido a que afuera solo está spitting Jim dejó su paraguas en casa.

Since it was only spitting outside, Jim left his umbrella at home.

El meteorólogo predijo pea soup fog para el día de mañana.

The weatherman forecasted pea soup fog for tomorrow.

F ill in the blanks with the appropriate idioms.

01 The little puddles left over after a rainstorm usually _____ up quickly in the sun.

Los pequeños charcos que quedan después de la lluvia usualmente se secan rápidamente con el sol.

02 The children were hoping the weather would _____ _____ so their baseball game would not be cancelled.

Los niños esperaban que el clima se despeje para que su partido de béisbol no se suspenda.

03 The golfers waited for the wind to _____ _____ before going back out onto the course.

Los golfistas esperaron que el viento disminuya antes de regresar al campo.

04 The weatherman said that we could be in for a _____ _____, so make sure you bring your jacket.

El meteorólogo dijo que se aproxima una ola de frío, así que asegúrense de llevar abrigos.

05 Jessica packed her umbrella and boots because it was supposed to _____ _____ and _____ later in the afternoon.

Jessica empacó su paraguas y sus botas porque era muy probable que lloviera a cántaros por la tarde.

06 It was not until later in August that the water would usually _____ _____ enough to go swimming in Canada.

Había que esperar hasta finales de agosto para que el agua aumentase de temperatura de manera que se pueda nadar en Canadá.

07 We could feel the air _____ _____ as the storm blew in.

Sentíamos el viento enfriarse mientras se avecinaba la tormenta.

08 Last summer was like one long _____ _____, so we kept our air conditioning on constantly.

El último verano hubo una prolongada ola de calor, por esa razón mantuvimos el aire acondicionado prendido constantemente.

09 Since it was only _____, we left the umbrella in the car.

Debido a que solo estaba chispeando, dejamos el paraguas en el carro.

10 As soon as we spread our blanket out on the beach, the sun disappeared and it began to _____ _____.

Tan pronto pusimos la cobija en la arena de la playa, el sol desapareció y comenzó a nublarse.

11 On the radio, the traffic reporter said that the haze was as thick as _____ _____, so drivers should go slowly.

En la radio, el reportero de tráfico dijo que la neblina estaba muy densa y los conductores debían conducir con cuidado.

12 It was _____ outside so Mom suggested that we all go swimming to _____ off.

Estaba húmedo afuera, por esa razón mamá sugirió que todos vayamos a nadar para refrescarnos.

13 Craig knew it was _____ weather when it started to snow in May.

Craig sabía que el clima estaba loco cuando comenzó a nevar en mayo.

14 The camping trip was ruined when it started to rain _____ on the campers and their tents.

El campamento se arruinó cuando comenzó a llover a cántaros sobre los campistas y sus carpas.

15 Alison knew there was _____ weather coming when the weatherman mentioned sleet and freezing rain.

Alison sabía que se aproximaba un clima terrible cuando el meteorólogo anunció aguanieve y lluvia congelada.

16 As she looked out her window and saw the rain _____ _____ in _____, Abigail knew the parade would be cancelled.

Mientras observaba por la ventana y vio el tremendo aguacero, Abigail sabía que el desfile se cancelaría.

Answers   1. dry (up) 2. clear up 3. die down 4. cold spell 5. rain cats (and) dogs 6. heat up 7. cool down 8. heat wave 9. spitting 10. cloud up 11. pea soup 12. sticky / cool (off) 13. crazy (weather) 14. (rain) buckets 15. killer (weather) 16. coming down (in) sheets

R ead the following story and refer to the questions below.

- Rain, Rain, Go Away

When he woke up, Ray looked out the window at the rain coming down in sheets and knew that it would not clear up by the end of the day. He had listened to the weather report the day before and heard the reporter say that it would start to cloud up overnight and the storm would hit around 7:00 am.

This would be the third weekend in a row that it rained buckets when he wanted to be out playing basketball with his friends. Last month he would have given anything for the weather to cool off. They had endured* two weeks of heat wave temperatures, and it had hardly even cooled down at night for sleeping. Lying in bed on those hot nights, Ray knew what his mom meant when she talked about sticky weather. That heat was killer weather, but the rain was not much better.

The reports had said that they were in for a bit of a cold spell, but they did not mention anything about it raining cats and dogs for three weekends in a row! Now, all Ray could do was wait and hope for the crazy weather to stop. The reports did say that the wind would die down by the next morning and it would only be spitting. Even so, it would take a day or two before all of the puddles* dried up at his favorite outdoor basketball court.

---

*endure soportar   *puddle charco

Questions about the story

1. What did Ray see when he looked out the window?
2. Did he think that the weather was going to clear up?
3. What did he hear the reporter say?
4. What was the weather like for the last two weekends?
5. What type of weather did Ray have last month?
6. What did he wish for last month?
7. What kind of weather would you say that Ray is experiencing?
8. How long would it take after the rain stops before Ray can go to his favorite outdoor basketball court and why?

Questions for discussion

1. What is the weather like today?
2. What type of weather do you enjoy the most? Why?
3. What kind of weather do you dislike the most? Why?
4. When was the last time that it rained cats and dogs? Were you stuck in it? Did you have an umbrella?
5. In your opinion, what is killer weather? When was the last time you experienced it?

Vete, lluvia, vete

Cuando despertó, Ray miró por la ventana y vio como caía un aguacero, entonces supo que no se iba a despejar sino hasta el final del día. El día anterior había escuchado el pronóstico del tiempo y el reportero dijo que comenzaría a nublarse por la noche y caería una tormenta alrededor de las 7:00 am. Esta sería la tercera semana consecutiva que llovería a cántaros cuando quería salir a jugar básquet con sus amigos. El mes pasado hubiera dado lo que fuese para que la temperatura baje. Habían soportado dos semanas la oleada de calor, y el calor casi no disminuía por las noches para poder dormir. Acostado en cama en esas noches de calor, Ray se dio cuenta de lo que le dijo su madre cuando mencionó el clima húmedo. Ese calor era despiadado, pero la lluvia no arreglaba las cosas.

Los reportes habían anunciado que se avecinaría una pequeña oleada de frío, pero no mencionaron nada sobre las lluvias a cántaros por tres semanas consecutivas. Ahora lo único que Ray podía hacer era aguantarse y esperar que el clima loco cese. Los reportes sí anunciaron que los vientos aminorarían para la mañana siguiente y que solo chispearía. Aun así, pasarían de uno a dos días hasta que los charcos se sequen en su cancha de básquet favorita.

Chapters ❶ - ❺

Review Chapters 1-5 and fill in the crossword below.

Answers ➜ P.172

Across

02. I'll be back in a _____, baby, so be ready at the door.

03. Studying hard every day will make me more successful in the _____ _____.

06. The weeklong sale at Macy's will _____ _____ Sunday.

11. Meg has a habit of starting things at the _____ _____ and always being late.

13. to come to an end; to finish

16. to intend to do something or start despite some interruption

18. We watched from the window as the rain came down _____ _____.

19. After two weeks of _____ _____ temperatures, the rain was a welcome sight.

21. to remain awake while waiting for a person to return home

22. Did you forget to brush your teeth? You've got _____ _____!

24. to sleep later than normal

Down

01. Pack your umbrella. It's supposed to rain _____ _____ _____ this afternoon.

03. I'm so tired. I will probably sleep _____ _____ _____ tonight.

04. Hey, don't leave yet. It's not over until the _____ _____ _____.

05. I'm going to _____ _____ _____ as soon as I get home tonight. I'm exhausted.

07. to fall asleep from exhaustion

08. The kids are so tired, they'll _____ _____ as soon as they lie down.

09. from the very beginning; with no help

10. to lose strength, lessen in power or weaken

12. daybreak

14. to not go to bed at the normal time

15. The water pipes in my house froze during the _____ _____ last year.

17. in a relatively short period of time; almost instantly

20. I'm going to excercise more and eat right. I'm turning over a new _____.

23. I was so tired that I didn't even hear the alarm _____ off.

Going to School

hit the books
to study earnestly.
estudiar meticulosamente.

Jane puso toda actividad a un lado para poder hit the books **sin distracciones.**
Jane put all other activities aside so she could hit the books without distraction.

brush up (on)
to re-familiarize oneself through review and study.
volver a familiarizarse mediante repaso y estudio.

Habiendo dejado a un lado por una semana los estudios de ciencia, Helen decidió brush up on **sus conocimientos científicos.**
Having put science studies aside for one week, Helen decided to brush up on her scientific knowledge.

cram
to study a large amount of material shortly before an examination.
estudiar una gran cantidad de material justo antes de alguna prueba.

Debido a que Gordon no hizo sus tareas todos los días tuvo que cram **la noche antes de la prueba.**
Gordon's failure to do his homework each day forced him to cram the night before the test.

pop quiz
a short surprise test.
pequeña prueba sorpresa.

Sin ninguna advertencia el profesor de ciencia tomó un pop quiz **al inicio de la clase.**
Without any warning, the science teacher gave the

class a pop quiz at the beginning of the day.

sign up
to join up; to enroll; to agree to do something.
suscribirse; inscribirse; participar.

Andy se emocionó cuando su madre lo sign up en el equipo de fútbol.
Andy was excited when his mother signed him up to play soccer.

handout
a document or paper to be distributed or given out.
documento o papel que se distribuye o entrega.
Verb hand out; pass out: to distribute or give out documents or papers.
distribuir o entregar un documento o papel.

Se adjuntó un handout a las instrucciones para entender mejor los procedimientos.
A handout was attached to the instructions to better understand the procedures.

bookworm
a person who reads a lot.
persona que lee mucho; ratón de biblioteca.

Mary es una bookworm, rara vez se la ve sin un libro.
Mary is such a bookworm that she is seldom seen without reading material.

hand in
to submit or offer something by hand.
entregar o devolver algo.
Synonym turn in.

Al final de la temporada todos en el equipo hand in sus uniformes.
At the end of the season, everyone on the team hands in their uniforms.

teacher's pet
a student who appears to be the teacher's favorite.
estudiante que al parecer es el preferido por el profesor.

Jimmy pensó convertirse en el teacher's pet trayendo una manzana a la profesora.
Jimmy thought he could become the teacher's pet by bringing her an apple.

flunk out
to drop out of school or quit attending school due to failing grades.
cesar estudios o dejar de asistir a la escuela debido a reprobar las materias.

Habiendo perdido interés en el curso, Sally se dio por vencida y flunk out de manera miserable.
Having lost interest in the course, Sally simply gave up and flunked out miserably.

drop out

to quit attending school; to abandon an activity without finishing it.

dejar de asistir a clases; abandonar una actividad sin completarla.

David drop out sus estudios para poder mantener a su familia.

David dropped out of school in order to support the family financially.

skip school

to not attend school for either part of or a whole day.

no asistir a clases ya sea por parte del día o día completo.

Synonym cut class; cut school; play hooky.

Debido a que el partido de fútbol era durante horas de clase, el estudiante decidió skip school e irse al partido.

Since the soccer game was during class hours, the student decided to skip school and go to the game.

ace

to score nearly perfectly or perfectly on a test; a person who is top in his or her field.

obtener nota perfecta o casi perfecta en una prueba; una persona que está sobre los demás en una materia o tema.

David ace su examen obteniendo nota perfecta.

David aced his exam with a perfect score.

F ill in the blanks with the appropriate idioms.

01 The students knew that they were to _____ in their book reports by 4:30 pm on the due date.

Los estudiantes sabían que tenían que entregar sus reportes a las 4:30pm, fecha tope.

02 The teacher chose two students each week to _____ _____ the assignments.

El profesor eligió a dos estudiantes para que todas las semanas repartan los documentos.

03 Maggie did not want to be labeled as a _____ _____ , so she chose to accept the same punishment as the other students even though she was absent when the misbehavior occurred.

Maggie no quería ser llamada "la preferida del profe", así que decidió recibir el mismo castigo que el resto de alumnos aun estando ella ausente cuando los hechos sucedieron.

04 Since Dee had worked long hours all week and did not have time to study, she had to _____ for the exam.

Debido a que Dee trabajó largas horas toda la semana y no tuvo tiempo para estudiar, tuvo que estudiar intensamente para el examen.

05 All students were required to _____ up _____ laboratory times coinciding with their biology class.

Todos los estudiantes debían inscribirse en laboratorio, junto con la clase de biología.

06 No one in the class was prepared for the _____ _____ on the first day back after the holiday.

Nadie en la clase estaba preparado para el examen sorpresa que se tomó el día justo después de feriados.

07 Simon scanned the pages of his textbook to _____ up _____ the chapter he was supposed to read the previous evening.

Simon escaneó las páginas de su libro para repasar el capítulo que debía haber leído la noche anterior.

08 Alan promised his parents he would hit _____ _____ on Friday instead of going out with his friends.

Alan prometió a sus padres que estudiaría el viernes en vez de salir con sus amigos.

09 Simon knew if he _____ out of school this time, his parents would be very upset.

Simon sabía que si reprobaba en la escuela, sus padres se enojarían mucho.

10 Burton and Michelle loved that their daughter Abigail was a _____ and was always reading two or three books a week.

A Burton y Michele les encantaba que su hija Abigail sea un ratón de biblioteca y leyese dos a tres libros por semana.

11 When all of his friends chose to _____ _____ on Friday afternoon, Casey resisted the pressure and went to class.

Cuando todos los amigos de Casey decidieron no ir a clases la tarde del viernes, Casey se resistió a la presión y fue a clases de todas maneras.

12 Once the marks were posted for the midterm exams, two or three students usually _____ out of school rather than continue studying.

Una vez calificados los exámenes trimestrales, dos a tres estudiantes usualmente se retiran de la escuela en lugar de seguir estudiando.

13 Linda's studying really paid off when she _____ all of her final exams.

Todo el estudio de Linda valió la pena cuando alcanzó la máxima nota en su examen final.

Answers   1. hand (in)   2. hand out   3. teacher's pet   4. cram   5. sign (up) for   6. pop quiz   7. brush (up) on   8. (hit) the books   9. flunked (out)   10. bookworm   11. skip school   12. dropped (out)   13. aced

Read the following story and refer to the questions below.

- Freshman Blues

Kara's entire last month of school had been a nightmare. She knew if she didn't hit the books soon she would have to drop out of school. She couldn't believe that she would have to end up cramming for all of her exams.

Kara had high hopes for herself. In high school, she had been the teacher's pet and had always handed in her assignments on time. She began the year by signing up for all of the toughest courses. In the past, Kara had never had any trouble brushing up on any subject just before an exam. She was used to skipping school, working a few extra hours at her job, and having a friend pick up any handouts she missed.

She had always thought of herself as a bookworm, not someone who would flunk out in her first year of college. During the pop quiz last week in psychology, Kara thought she had done well, but her mark turned out to be below the class average. Kara knew she might have to rethink her career path.

Questions about the story

1. What kind of time was Kara having at school last month?
2. What kind of pressure is she facing?
3. How is she studying?
4. What kind of a student is Kara?
5. What did Kara usually do?
6. Why is Kara worried about her schooling?

Questions for discussion

1. What kind of a student are you?
2. Do you know anybody who flunked out of school?
3. Did you or do you cram before tests? Why? Is this a good way to study?
4. Did you or do you ever skip school? Why?
5. Were you ever the teacher's pet?
6. What is something that you need to brush up on?

Pesares del primer año universitario

El mes pasado había sido una pesadilla para Kara. Sabía que si no se ponía a estudiar pronto tendría que dejar la escuela. No se imaginó que terminaría estudiando intensamente para poder pasar todas sus pruebas.

Kara tenía grandes expectativas s para sí misma. En el colegio, había sido la preferida del profesor y siempre había entregado sus deberes a tiempo. Inició el año inscribiéndose en todas las materias difíciles. En el pasado, Kara no había tenido ningún problema en estudiar y nivelarse para cualquier examen; solía saltarse clases, trabajar algunas horas extras y hacer que algún amigo recogiera los documentos que no había recibido.

Siempre se consideró un ratón de biblioteca, no como alguien que reprobaría su primer año universitario. Durante el examen sorpresa en psicología la semana pasada, Kara creyó que le había ido bien pero su calificación resultó ser inferior al promedio de toda la clase; Kara supo que tendría que reconsiderar si había elegido la profesión correcta.

Gone Shopping

window shop
to view items in store window displays without buying.
mirar la vitrina de una tienda sin comprar.

Sandra se vio forzada a window shop porque no tenía dinero.

Sandra was forced to window shop because she did not have any money.

shop around
to compare various qualities and functions of items at several stores before buying.
ir a algunas tiendas para comparar precios, cualidades y funciones antes de comprar.

El papá de Benjamin le advirtió que shop around antes de comprar un auto.

Benjamin was cautioned by his father to shop around before purchasing an automobile.

pick up
to buy without considerable thought; to purchase in a casual, unplanned way.
comprar sin pensar mucho; comprar de una manera inconsecuente y sin planificación.

Si vamos a comer hamburguesas luego, vamos a tener que pick up unos panes ahora.

If we are going to eat hamburgers later, we will have to pick up some buns now.

be sold out (of)
to have none of a certain item left.
agotarse un producto.

La tienda de Samir be sold out de palas de nieve el día posterior a la tormenta de nieve.

Samir's store was sold out of snow shovels the day

after the big snowstorm blew in.

on sale
available to purchase at a discounted price.
disponible para la venta a un precio rebajado.
Verb go on sale.
poner en remate.

Antes de que termine cada estación, la tienda liquida el inventario poniendo todo on sale.

Before each season ends, this clothing shop gets rid of old stock by putting everything on sale.

snap up
to buy or get something quickly and enthusiastically because it is cheap or exactly what you want.
comprar o conseguir algo rápido y con entusiasmo porque es barato o exactamente lo que quieres.

Mientras estaba de descuento el salmón, Sunny snap up lo más que pudo.

While the salmon was on sale, Sunny snapped up as much as she could.

hunt for bargains
to actively look for cheaper, lower priced items.
buscar cosas más baratas, con un menor precio.

Como quedaba poco dinero al final de cada mes, Barbara siempre tenía que hunt for bargains en el supermercado.

There was little money left at the end of each month so Barbara always had to hunt for bargains in the grocery store.

*Someone who hunts for bargains is called a bargain hunter.
Alguien que busca mejores precios, se llama un "bargain hunter".

pick out
to choose or select an item among a number of items.
elegir una cosa entre varias.

Ya que Grace había trabajado más tiempo por su jefe, los otros trabajadores le pidieron que ella pick out un regalo de cumpleaños para él.

Since Grace had worked for her boss the longest, the rest of the workers asked her to pick out a birthday gift for him.

stock up (on)
to buy items in bulk for later use.
comprar cosas por mayor para utilizar luego.

Mamá stock up latas de caldo de pollo antes de que llegara la temporada de frío.

Mom stocked up on canned chicken broth before the upcoming cold season.

buy up
to buy as many items as possible.
comprar todos los artículos posibles.

Andrew siempre buy up las bananas excesivamente maduras en el mercado de la esquina cuando las ponían de oferta.

Andrew would always buy up the overripe bananas at the corner grocery store when they went on sale.

*This idiom is mostly used when items are on sale or listed at a very low price. Este modismo se utiliza mayormente cuando hay artículos de oferta o con un precio muy bajo.

take back
to return an item to the place of purchase.
devolver un artículo al lugar donde se compró.

Dan take back el suéter porque no le gustó el color.

Dan took back the sweater because he did not like the color.

rain check
a promissory check provided by a place of business to the shopper that agrees to provide a currently sold-out sale item for the same sale price at a later date.
pagaré entregado al comprador por un negocio, mediante el cual se acuerda entregar luego, un artículo actualmente agotado al mismo precio de oferta.

Judy solicitó un rain check después de descubrir que los pollos congelados anunciados en oferta se habían acabado.

Judy asked for a rain check after she discovered that the frozen chickens advertised on sale were all gone.

F ill in the blanks with the appropriate idioms.

01 While he was on his way home, Alvin remembered he had to _____ _____ a few little things at the store.

Cuando estaba de camino a casa, Alvin recordó que tenía que recoger algunas cosas de la tienda.

02 Sandy and her mom loved to go to the mall on Saturdays to _____ _____ _____ .

A Sandy y su mamá les encantaba ir al centro comercial los sábados a mirar vitrinas.

03 Since he wanted to be sure he was getting a good deal, Jon decided to shop _____ before he purchased the video equipment.

Ya que quería estar seguro que era lo más barato que podía encontrar, Jon decidió comparar precios antes de comprar el equipo de video.

04 Mary decided to _____ up all of the hats at the craft show, because she knew she could sell them for more at the mall.

Mary decidió comprar de todos los sombreros en el festival de artesanías porque sabía que los podía vender por más en el centro comercial.

05 As the millennium was approaching, many people _____ up _____ water and batteries for their homes.

Al acercarse el Nuevo Milenio, mucha gente se abasteció de agua y baterías para sus casas.

06 Alan tried hard to pick _____ a sweater that his wife would like.

Alan se esforzó mucho en elegir un suéter que le gustara a su esposa.

07 The electronics store had sold out of the video cameras they had advertised, so Paul asked for a _____ _____ .

En la tienda de electrónicos se habían agotado las cámaras de video que habían anunciado, por lo que Paul pidió un vale.

08 David planned to _____ _____ the hat he received from his brother, since it did not fit properly.

David decidió devolver el sombrero que le dio su hermano porque no le quedaba bien.

09 My mom loves to go downtown during the holidays to _____ _____ and to see how the stores have decorated.

A mi mamá le encanta ir al centro durante las fiestas para mirar vitrinas y ver cómo están decoradas las tiendas.

10 Nana's bakery makes the best pies every Sunday morning, so people are always there early to _____ up one or two for their families.

La panadería de Nana prepara los mejores pasteles cada domingo en la mañana, por lo que siempre hay gente allí temprano para echarle mano a uno o dos para sus familias.

11 Katie was waiting for the shoes she wanted to go _____ _____ before

she purchased them.
Katie estaba esperando que los zapatos que quería estuvieran de oferta para comprarlos.

12 **It did not take long for all of the stores in town to be _____ _____ of the hottest item this year.**
No tomó mucho tiempo para que en todas las tiendas del pueblo se hubiera agotado el artículo más popular del año.

Answers 1. pick up 2. hunt for bargains 3. (shop) around 4. buy (up) 5. stocked (up) on 6. (pick) out 7. rain check 8. take back 9. window shop 10. snap (up) 11. on sale 12. (be) sold out (of)

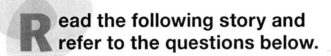

Read the following story and refer to the questions below.

- Good Buys

The holiday season was barely over and already Mia and Cindy were ready to get out again and hunt for bargains. Mia knew what she wanted and where to get it, so she didn't want to waste time shopping around for the best price. Neither Mia nor Cindy liked to window shop because they hated the idea of watching someone else snap up a great deal.

Both women had sweaters they had received from their husbands that they planned to take back and exchange for something else. Mia and Cindy were hoping to pick up a few extra things on sale while they were at the mall. The sweater that Mia had seen in an advertisement on the weekend was sold out, so she asked the clerk for a rain check.

Many stores had stocked up on the year's hottest new fad*, leg warmers. Now that they were overstocked*, merchants were hoping the teenagers would buy up at least one of each color they had available before they all disappeared. Mia and Cindy decided to pick out a few pairs of leg warmers for their daughters since they were selling for such a good price.

---

*fad moda pasajera *overstock exceso de inventario

Questions about the story

1. What time of year is it in the story?

2. Why are Mia and Cindy shopping after the holiday season?

3. Did the two shop around? Why?

4. Why do they dislike window shopping?

5. What were they going to do with the sweaters they received as gifts?

6. Why did Mia ask for a rain check?

7. What did the store stock up on?

Questions for discussion

1. Do you like to window shop? Why or why not?

2. During a flood or time of emergency, what kinds of food are snapped up?

3. Is it easy to take back items bought in your country? Explain.

4. Have you ever bought up all available items?

5. Does your country have a rain check policy?

6. What are some things that you might pick up while shopping?

7. What is a common item that many families stock up on in your country?

Buenas compras

Apenas habían terminado las fiestas y Mia y Cindy ya estaban listas para salir nuevamente en busca de ofertas. Mia sabía lo que quería y dónde conseguirlo, así que no quería perder tiempo comparando precios. Ni a Mia ni a Cindy les gustaba mirar vitrinas porque les desagradaba la idea de ver que alguien más le echaba mano a una gran oferta. Ambas mujeres habían recibido de sus esposos suéteres que decidieron devolver y cambiar por otra cosa. Mia y Cindy esperaban comprar algunas otras cosas de oferta mientras estaban en el centro comercial. El suéter que Mia había visto en un anuncio del fin de semana estaba agotado, por lo que pidió un vale al dependiente.

Muchas tiendas se habían abastecido de la moda más popular del año: calentadores de pierna. Ahora que tenían un exceso de inventario, los comerciantes esperaban que las adolescentes compraran al menos uno de cada color disponible antes de que todos desaparecieran. Mia y Cindy decidieron elegir algunos pares para sus hijas porque estaban a un precio muy bueno.

Traffic, Travel & Turns

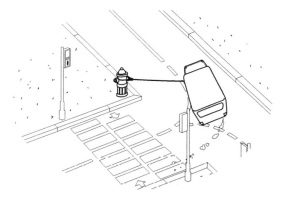

turn around
to reverse the direction of movement.
invertir la dirección del movimiento.

turn around**! Acabas de pasar el estacionamiento.**
Turn around! You just passed the parking ramp.

hang a left/right
to make a left/right turn.
girar a la izquierda/derecha.

hang a left **donde el semáforo y ve recto tres cuadras hasta la iglesia.**
Hang a left at the light and go straight three blocks to the church.

up to speed
moving at normal speeds; going the speed limit.
moverse a velocidad normal; conducir a la velocidad máxima.

Íbamos despacio por un rato, pero ahora por fin estamos up to speed**.**
It was slow for a while, but now we finally got up to speed.

run a (red) light
to go through a red light without stopping.
pasarse la luz roja. España: saltarse el semáforo.

Harry run a light **cuando llevaba a su esposa embarazada al hospital.**
Harry ran a light taking his pregnant wife to the hospital.

as far as
up until a certain place.
hasta llegar a un cierto lugar.

Voy a ir as far as **la escuela. ¿Me puedes llevar?**
I'm going as far as the school. Can you give me a lift?

pull over
to drive to the side of the road and stop or cause to do so.
conducir hasta el lado de la carretera y detenerse; orillarse.

pull into
to leave the road to park.
salir de la carretera para estacionarse; ingresar.

make a wrong turn
to turn at the wrong place.
girar en el lugar incorrecto.

make a U-turn
to turn in the shape of a U; to reverse direction.
dar vuelta en U.

bumper-to-bumper
traffic that is so congested the car bumpers are only inches away from one another.
tráfico tan congestionado que los parachoques de los carros están a solo centímetros uno del otro.

stop and go
traffic that moves in starts and stops; not free flowing.
tráfico que se mueve un poco y se detiene, no se mueve libremente; tráfico de tire y afloje; tráfico intermitente.

---

pull over para que pueda mirar lo que pasa con el carro.
Pull over, so I can see what's wrong with the car.

Vamos a pull into esa gasolinera. Estamos con el tanque vacío.
Let's pull into that gas station just ahead. We're on empty.
Often followed by parking lot, driveway, gas station, garage or other place to stop the car.
A menudo seguido por 'parking lot' (estacionamiento), 'driveway' (entrada), 'gas station' (gasolinera), 'garage' (garaje) u otro lugar donde se pueda estacionar un carro.

Cada vez que Ben intenta encontrar la casa de Jon, el make a wrong turn y se pierde.
Every time Ben tries to find Jon's house, he makes a wrong turn and gets lost.

Está bien, make a U-turn por aquí y la oficina estará a tu derecha.
OK, make a U-turn up here and the office will be on your right.

Debes esperar trafico bumper-to-bumper en las carreteras principales durante el Día de Gracias.
You should expect bumper-to-bumper traffic on the major highways over Thanksgiving.

Es stop-and-go en el autopista hasta LA hoy de mañana.
It's stop-and-go on the freeway into LA this morning.
This idiom is hyphenated when used before a noun as an adjective.
En este modismo, las palabras están unidas con un guion cuando se utiliza como adjetivo, antes de un sustantivo.

gridlock
a traffic jam that allows for no
progress in any direction.
atasco de tráfico que no permite
moverse en ninguna dirección;
congestión; embotellamiento.

fender bender
a collision between cars with only
minor damage.
choque entre carros con pocos
daños; un golpecito. España:
accidente mínimo.

El accidente dejó la intersección en gridlock por una hora.
The accident left the intersection gridlocked for an hour.

Jasmine tuvo un fender bender no muy serio anoche, pero está bien.
Jasmine was in a minor fender bender last night, but she's all right.

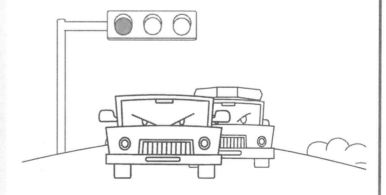

F ill in the blanks with the appropriate idioms.

01 Whenever there is a _____, Jeff leaves his car at home and goes to work by subway because he knows that traffic won't be moving at all.

Cuando hay un atasco de carros, Jeff deja su carro en casa y va al trabajo en metro porque sabe que el tráfico no se moverá en lo absoluto.

02 The police _____ me _____ for speeding and gave me a ticket.

La policía me detuvo por exceso de velocidad y me dio una multa.

03 If you want to find the library, go _____ _____ _____ the river and turn left.

Si quieres encontrar la biblioteca, sigue hasta llegar al río y gira a la izquierda.

04 Driving in _____ - and - _____ traffic can be quite frustrating.

Manejar en tráfico intermitente puede ser muy frustrante.

05 Robin pulled _____ the driveway to park.

Robin ingresó al camino de entrada para estacionarse.

06 With the big delivery truck, it was hard to _____ _____ on the small streets.

Con el camión grande, era muy difícil dar la vuelta en las calles pequeñas.

07 After driving in an hour of congested traffic, we were all happy to get on the highway and get _____ to _____.

Después de manejar por una hora en el tráfico congestionado, estamos todos felices de llegar a la autopista y obtener la velocidad máxima.

08 The police pulled me over for _____ a _____.

La policía me detuvo por pasar la luz roja.

09 Jon _____ _____ right at the intersection, when he should have gone left.

Jon giró a la derecha en la intersección cuando debió haberse ido a la izquierda.

10 Ralph made _____ _____ turn on the way to his best friend's wedding and ended up arriving late.

Ralph giró incorrectamente cuando estaba yendo al matrimonio de su mejor amigo y terminó llegando tarde.

11 It's right there on the other side of the street. Just _____ a _____ - _____ and park.

Esta allí al otro lado de la calle. Simplemente da la vuelta en U y estaciónate.

12 It may have only been a _____ _____, but my neck really hurts.

Tal vez solo fue un golpecito, pero mi cuello me duele mucho.

13 With _____ - to - _____ traffic, it takes Claude an hour to get to school every day.

Con el trafico parachoques contra parachoques, Claude demora una hora para llegar a la escuela todos los días.

Answers 1. gridlock 2. pulled (me) over 3. as far as 4. stop-(and)-go 5. (pulled) into 6. turn around 7. up (to) speed 8. running (a) light 9. hung a (right) 10. (made) a wrong (turn) 11. make (a) U-turn 12. fender bender 13. bumper-(to)-bumper

Read the following story and refer to the questions below.

- Running Late

Nothing is worse than getting pulled over for a moving violation* when you're late for something. The fact that Greg was speeding was reason enough for the police to pull him over, but Greg didn't see it that way.

The whole day had been a mess. First, he left the house early to avoid the bumper-to-bumper congestion on the highway, only to find his alternate route gridlocked. It seems someone had run a light and caused a fender-bender.

He made a quick U-turn to get out of it, but got all turned around and made a wrong turn. Then he got stuck in stop-and-go traffic. The first time he had gotten up to speed was when the police caught him in a speed trap. The cop took his time writing out the ticket. Finally, he got as far as the school and hung a right. When he pulled into the school parking lot, the other students were coming out of the building. The test was over!!

*moving violation infracción de circulación.

Questions about the story

1. Why did Greg get pulled over?
2. Why did he leave the house early? Did his plan work?
3. Why was the road gridlocked?
4. How did Greg get out of the gridlock?
5. What happened after that?
6. When did he get up to speed?
7. When did he hang a right?
8. What did he see when he pulled into the school parking lot?

Questions for discussion

1. What made Greg think he shouldn't be pulled over? What do you think?
2. What are the laws for speeding in your country? Are they enforced?
3. How is the traffic in your country at different times of the day?
4. What do you do when you're in bumper-to-bumper traffic?
5. Have you ever been in a fender bender? How was it resolved?
6. Describe how you get to work (in detail).

Llegando tarde

No hay nada peor que la policía te detenga por alguna infracción cuando estás atrasado. El hecho es que Greg estaba conduciendo demasiado rápido, razón suficiente para que la policía lo detuviera, pero Greg no lo vio así.

Todo el día había sido un desastre. Primero, salió de la casa temprano para evitar la congestión en la autopista, pero encontró su ruta alternativa con tráfico. Parece que alguien se había pasado la luz roja y causado un pequeño choque. Greg dio vuelta en U para salir del tráfico, pero dio una vuelta equivocada. Por eso quedó atrapado en tráfico de tire y afloje. La primera vez en que al fin obtuvo velocidad de crucero fue cuando la policía lo agarró con un detector de velocidad. La policía tomó su tiempo en hacerle la multa. Finalmente, llegó hasta la escuela y giró a la derecha. Cuando ingresó al estacionamiento de la escuela, los otros estudiantes estaban saliendo del edificio. ¡Se había acabado el examen!

Dining

grab a bite
to eat something quickly while on the go.
comer algo rápido y en el camino.

En vez de almorzar, Bill grab a bite camino a la escuela.
Instead of stopping for lunch, Bill grabbed a bite on his way to school.

eat out
to eat at a restaurant.
comer en un restaurante.

John decidió eat out en un café en el centro.
John decided to eat out at a café downtown.

leftovers
the food remaining after a meal.
las sobras de comida.

Craig otra vez estaba con hambre a media noche, por lo que comió las leftovers de la celebración familiar.
At midnight Craig was hungry again, so he ate the leftovers from the family celebration.

*In western culture, it is common to make more food than needed and to eat leftovers for a snack or another meal. During the holiday season a lot of food is cooked, and families often eat leftovers for days to come.
En la cultura occidental, es común preparar mas comida de lo necesario y comer las sobras. Durante las fiestas, se prepara mucha comida y las familias comen sobras por muchos dias.

takeout
hot cooked food that you buy at a store or restaurant to eat somewhere else.

Gordon recogerá una pizza takeout para cenar en casa.
Gordon will pick up takeout pizza for supper at home.

*When ordering at a restaurant the service clerk will sometimes ask "Is

comida caliente comprada en una tienda o restaurante para comer en otra parte.
Synonym carryout.
Verb to take out.

junk food
unhealthy food that is quick and easy to eat.
comida no saludable que es fácil y rápida de comer; comida chatarra.

potluck
an informal meal where each guest brings a prepared dish of food.
cena en que cada persona trae un plato de comida.

have a craving for
to have a strong or uncontrollable desire for something.
estar antojado de algo.
Synonym crave for.

pig out
to eat too much food; to eat like an animal.
comer demasiada comida; comer como un cerdo.

wolf down
to eat food quickly (often without chewing).
devorar la comida (a veces sin masticar).
Synonym gulp down.

doggy bag
a small bag or container that a restaurant supplies customers with to take unfinished food home.

this for here or to go?" In this case, the words 'to go' mean food that is to be taken out of the restaurant. 'To go' is used at the time of ordering food only. Cuando se pide comida en un restaurante, a veces te preguntarán: "¿Es para servirse aquí o para llevar?" En este caso, las palabras 'to go' (para llevar) significan comida que vas a llevar fuera del restaurante.

Papas fritas y cola son junk food muy agradable.
Potato chips and cola are enjoyable junk food snacks.

Benjamin llevó verduras y Mary llevó un postre a la cena potluck.
Benjamin took vegetables and Mary took a dessert to the potluck dinner.

Cuando Betty estaba embarazada con su primer hijo, have a craving for helados y galletas.
When Betty was pregnant with her first child, she had a craving for ice cream and cookies.

La comida estaba tan buena que Jim pig out y comió más de lo que debía.
The food was so good that Jim pigged out and ate more than his fair share.

Después de practicar fútbol, Tony tenía tanta hambre que wolf down su comida, casi sin respirar entre bocados.
After football practice, Tony was so hungry that he wolfed down his food, hardly taking a breath between bites.

Pete no pudo acabar su comida y pidió un doggy bag para llevar las sobras a la casa.

bolsitas o contenedores de un restaurante para llevar la comida que sobra; bolsita de sobras para el perro.

Pete could not finish his meal and asked the waiter for a doggy bag so he could take the unfinished portion home.

have a sweet tooth
to enjoy eating sweet food and candies.
Disfrutar comer dulces y caramelos; ser goloso.

Las visitas al dentista siempre son más costosas si uno have a sweet tooth.

Visits to a dentist are always more costly if one has a sweet tooth.

eat up
to entirely consume all of the food available.
consumir completamente toda la comida; comerse todo. España: rebanar el plato.

Johnny tenía tanta hambre que eat up todo lo que veía.

Johnny was so hungry that he ate up everything in sight.

F ill in the blanks with the appropriate idioms.

01 On Saturdays, Mom usually serves _____ from Friday night for dinner.

Los sábados, mamá normalmente sirve las sobras de la comida del viernes.

02 As people stepped up to the counter to order their food, Paula asked them if they wanted _____.

Cuando la gente llegaba a la barra para pedir su comida, Paula les preguntaba si querían comida para llevar.

03 After her meal at the restaurant, Tammy asked for a _____ bag to take home what she could not finish.

Después de comer en el restaurante, Tammy pidió una bolsita de sobras para llevar lo que no podía comer.

04 Neither Ian nor Ray felt like making supper, so they decided to _____ _____.

Ni Ian ni Ray quisieron preparar la cena, entonces decidieron comer fuera.

05 Grandma always insisted that we _____ _____ everything on our plates and not waste a bite.

La abuela siempre insistía que comiéramos todo lo que está en nuestro plato y no desperdiciar nada.

06 Since she _____ a _____ tooth, Maggie always had a dish of candy at her desk.

Ya que ella es muy golosa, Maggie siempre tiene un plato de caramelos en su escritorio.

07 All of the teachers at school brought a dish of food for the holiday _____ luncheon.

Todos los profesores en la escuela trajeron un plato de comida para el almuerzo.

08 Damon chose not to eat any more _____ _____ once his pants started to get too tight.

Damon decidió no comer más comida chatarra cuando se dio cuenta de que sus pantalones le comenzaban a quedar más apretados.

09 Dwayne was late for basketball practice, so he had to _____ _____ his breakfast before he headed out the door.

Dwayne estaba atrasado para la práctica de básquet, por eso tuvo que devorar su desayuno antes de salir de casa.

10 While he went to get more dip, Josh hoped his sister would not _____ _____ on the rest of the chips.

Mientras iba por más salsa, Josh esperaba que su hermana no fuera a comer como un cerdo el resto de las papas fritas.

11 Since the commercial came on, Eva has _____ a _____ for potato chips all evening.

Después de mirar el anuncio, Eva tuvo antojo de papas fritas toda la noche.

12 Dan would often skip breakfast at home and _____ a _____ to eat on the way to work at the local sandwich shop.

A menudo, Dan no desayunaba en casa y comía algo en su camino al trabajo.

Answers 1. leftovers 2. takeout 3. doggy (bag) 4. eat out 5. eat up 6. had (a) sweet (tooth) 7. potluck 8. junk food 9. wolf down 10. pig out 11. had (a) craving (for) 12. grab (a) bite

Read the following story and refer to the questions below.

- The Takeout Twins

Burton and Jewel hated to cook. Their refrigerator contained only the bare necessities* and takeout food containers with leftovers. Usually, they would eat up all their leftovers for lunch the next day. They spent half of the week eating out and taking home doggy bags, and the other half ordering takeout for supper in front of the TV. Even when Burton and Jewel were involved in potluck luncheons at work, they would order a tray of food, instead of taking the time to cook something in their own kitchen.

On the weekends, Burton loved to pig out on junk food while watching football on television. He could usually wolf down an entire bag of chips before halftime*. Jewel, on the other hand, had a sweet tooth, so she often had a craving for chocolate and ice cream while she watched television.

*bare necessities lo básico   *halftime descanso

Questions about the story

1. What does Burton and jewel's refrigerator have inside it?
2. When do they usually eat the leftovers?
3. How would they eat their dinners during the week?
4. What were Burton and Jewel involved in at work?
5. What did Burton love to do on the weekends?
6. How fast would Burton wolf down a bag of chips?
7. Does Jewel like to eat salty foods?
8. What does Jewel have a craving for?

Questions for discussion

1. Do you eat leftovers at home? If yes, what?
2. Do you have any special cravings for food when you are sad or depressed?
3. When was the last time that you pigged out on junk food? What did you eat?
4. Do you have a sweet tooth? What do you enjoy eating?
5. When is it OK to ask for a doggy bag and when is it not OK?
6. Do you usually take your time to eat, or do you wolf down your food?

La pareja que solo pedía comida para llevar

Burton y Jewel odiaban cocinar. Su refrigeradora tenía solamente lo básico y contenedores de comida con sobras. Normalmente, comían todas las sobras para el almuerzo del día siguiente. Pasaban la mitad de la semana comiendo fuera y llevando bolsitas de sobras y la otra mitad de la semana pidiendo comida para cenar mientras veían la televisión. Incluso, cuando Burton y Jewel debían llevar al trabajo comida para compartirla con los demás, la compraban en vez de preparar algo en casa.

Los fines de semana, a Burton le gustaba comer como un cerdo comida chatarra mientras veía futbol en la televisión. Normalmente, devoraba una bolsa entera de papas fritas antes del primer tiempo del partido. Por otro lado, Jewel era muy golosa y normalmente tenía antojos de chocolate y helado mientras veía la televisión.

Housewrk

Housework 10

idiomATTACK

Quehaceres Domésticos

take out
to remove from the house;
to get rid of.
sacar algo de la casa.

Me gustaría take out la pared y poner una puerta de vidrio enorme aquí.

I would like to take out this wall and place a giant sliding glass door here instead.

*This idiom is often used when referring to garbage, recycling and other similarly unwanted items.
Ese modismo se utiliza normalmente para referirse a basura, reciclaje, y otras cosas para desechar.

clean up
to clean by organizing or removing dust or dirt from objects; to make neat.
limpiar removiendo suciedad y polvo de los objetos; dejar limpio.

Tengo que clean up el desorden que hizo mi hermanito en el piso.

I have to clean up the mess that my little brother made on the floor.

pick up
to clean by picking up objects that were left carelessly and organizing them.
recoger cosas botadas y organizarlas.

Tengo que llegar a casa y pick up la casa antes de que mis papás lleguen y encuentren el desorden que hicimos mis amigos y yo.

I have to hurry home and pick up the house before my parents see the mess my friends and I made.

straighten up
to arrange neatly; to place in proper order.
arreglar la casa.
Synonym tidy up.

Mi esposa y yo necesitamos straighten up la casa antes de que lleguen los invitados.

My wife and I need to quickly straighten up the house before our guests arrive.

make food
to prepare or cook a meal.
preparar comida.
Synonym make breakfast; make lunch; make dinner; make a snack.

¿Quién va a make food si tus papás se van por una semana?

Who will make food if your parents go away for a week?

*'Cooking' implies that heat is to be used, whereas 'making' does not clarify any distinction.
'cooking' implica que se utiliza fuego, mientras 'making' no hace esta distinción.

do the dishes
to wash dirty dishes after a meal.
lavar los platos.

Jason, Tyler y Matthew trabajaron a prisa para do the dishes antes de que empezara su programa de televisión favorito.

Jason, Tyler and Matthew worked quickly to do the dishes before their favorite television program started.

fix up
to repair cosmetically; to fix to working order.
arreglar algo para que funcione.

Chris compró un nuevo carro y quiso fix up. Dijo que cambiaría un poco el interior y polarizaría los vidrios.

Chris bought a new car and planned to fix it up. He said that he would tint the windows and change some of the interior.

*This idiom generally refers to improving something's appearance.
Este modismo se refiere a mejorar el aspecto de algo.

clean house
to do the needed chores around the house; to maintain the house; to do housework.
limpiar la casa; mantener la casa; hacer las tareas de casa.

Sara se quedó en casa durante su día libre para clean house.

Sarah stayed home on her day off so that she could clean house.

odds and ends
several unfinished or little jobs that need to be done.
trabajos pequeños que deben ser terminados.

Este fin de semana, tengo que quedarme en casa y hacer algunos odds and ends que mi esposa me ha estado pidiendo que haga durante las últimas dos semanas.

This weekend, I have to stay home and complete a few odds and ends that my wife has been asking me to do for the past two weeks.

*'Odds and ends' are not chores that happen on a regular basis.
'Odds and ends' no son trabajos de casa que se deben hacer todos los días.

garage sale
a special sale held in front of

El Sr. Paven realiza un garage sale cada año para vender sus cosas viejas.

one's house or garage, selling used items no longer wanted or needed. venta especial en frente de la casa o dentro del garaje, vender cosas usadas que ya no se desean o necesitan.
*Synonym yard sale.

clean out
to clean something by removing unnecessary items.
vaciar algo sacando cosas que ya no sirven o se utilizan.

spring cleaning
a thorough or extensive cleaning of a house.
limpieza profunda de la casa.

put something back
to return an object to its proper place.
regresar algo a su lugar; devolver.
*Synonym put away.

keep house
to maintain consistent care of a house; to do the cooking and cleaning.
cuidar una casa; hacer la limpieza y cocina.

upkeep
the process of keeping something in good condition.
mantener en buen estado.

Mr. Paven has a garage sale every year in order to get rid of some of his old junk.

*These are articles that one no longer needs or simply wants to sell for profit. The holder of the garage sale places all of the goods in his or her garage or in front of his or her house. When several families do this together it is called a 'block sale'.
Se trata de artículos que ya nadie necesita o que simplemente se venden para ganar algo de dinero. El vendedor pone todas las cosas que quiere vender dentro del garaje o frente a su casa. Cuando algunas familias lo hacen juntas, se llama 'block sale'.

Mi esposa me dijo que tengo que clean out el closet porque está lleno de chatarra.

My wife told me that I have to clean out the storage closet because it was filled with junk.

*This idiom is mainly used for closets, drawers and refrigerators, but is not limited to this usage only.
Este modismo se utiliza normalmente para closets, cajones y refrigeradores, pero no solamente en estos casos.

Mi familia quiere que me quede en casa este fin de semana para ayudarles a hacer un poco de spring cleaning.

My family wants me to stay home this weekend and help them do some spring cleaning.

*'Spring cleaning' can happen regardless of the season but is usually done at the end of winter.
'Spring cleaning' puede ocurrir durante cualquier temporada del año, pero normalmente se hace al final del invierno.

No te olvides de put my book back después de acabarlo.

Don't forget to put my book back after you're finished with it.

Fred estaba impresionado con la habilidad de Linda, su nueva esposa para keep house.

Fred was impressed with how his new wife, Linda, could keep house.

Aunque la grande y vieja casa de campo necesitaba bastante upkeep, Troy y Kelly decidieron comprarla.

Even though the large old farmhouse would require a lot of upkeep, Troy and Kelly decided to buy it.

F ill in the blanks with the appropriate idioms.

01 Julie did not want to do _____ _____ until after the guests had left because she thought that it might be rude.

Julie no quiso lavar los platos hasta que se fueran los invitados porque pensaba que era de mala educación.

02 Tim and Michelle stopped at a _____ _____ on Saturday morning to look for baby items.

Tim y Michelle pararon en una venta de garaje el sábado en la mañana a buscar cosas para bebés.

03 The guests were arriving soon, so Joanne asked her children to _____ _____ their rooms.

Los invitados iban a llegar pronto, por eso Joanne pidió a sus hijos que limpiasen sus cuartos.

04 Wayne just had a few _____ _____ _____ to take care of around the house before he could go golfing.

Wayne solamente tenía que hacer algunos trabajos en casa antes de que pudiera ir a jugar golf.

05 Something had gone bad inside it, so Donna decided to _____ _____ the refrigerator.

Algo se había malogrado por eso Donna decidió vaciar la refrigeradora.

06 Mom always told us to _____ _____ everything where we found it when we were done playing.

Mamá siempre nos dijo que regresáramos todo a su lugar cuando hayamos terminado de jugar.

07 When staying home with the children all day, part of what Robin needed to do was _____ _____.

Cuando Robin se quedaba en casa todo el día con los niños, parte de su trabajo era cuidar la casa.

08 Shawn made sure he had all of the ingredients he needed to _____ food for his guests.

Shawn se aseguró de tener todos los ingredientes que necesitaba para preparar la comida para sus invitados.

09 The large piece of property would require a lot of _____ to maintain its neat and tidy appearance.

La propiedad grande requeriría mucho mantenimiento para que se vea limpia y arreglada.

10 Peter's job each Friday was to _____ _____ the garbage before school.

El trabajo de Peter todos los viernes era sacar la basura antes de ir a la escuela.

11 Bill had to _____ _____ the basement so they could use it as an extra bedroom.

Bill tenía que arreglar el sótano para que lo puedan utilizar como un cuarto extra.

12 The boys helped their mother _____ _____ on Saturday morning.

Los niños ayudaron a su mamá a limpiar la casa el sábado por la mañana.

13 When the glass lampshade shattered, we helped _____ up all of the pieces.

Cuando la lámpara de vidrio se rompió, ayudamos a recoger todos los pedazos.

14 Travis knew that he should _____ up his room before his grandparents arrived.

Travis sabía que tenía que arreglar su cuarto antes de que lleguen sus abuelos.

15 Every year, on the first warm weekend in April, Grandma opened the windows and did some _____ _____.

Cada año, en abril, durante el primer fin de semana de calor, la abuela abría las ventanas y hacía una limpieza profunda.

Answers 1. (do) the dishes 2. garage sale 3. clean up 4. odds and ends 5. clean out 6. put back 7. keep house 8. make (food) 9. upkeep 10. take out 11. fix up 12. clean house 13. pick (up) 14. straighten (up) 15. spring cleaning

Read the following story and refer to the questions below.

- Visiting Relatives

Sunday was the day our family usually went to visit Grandma and Grandpa. Grandma sure could keep house as it always looked immaculate*. We would usually go to their house after we ate breakfast. Dad helped Mom make the food, and we all sat down at the table to enjoy it. After breakfast, we helped Mom clean up the kitchen while Dad packed the car for our trip.

Since it was my turn to do the dishes, I started on them right away. Mom asked Stephen to take out the garbage and help Dad clean out the trunk so there would be room for our things. Once all of the dishes had been put back to where they belonged and the car was packed, we were on our way.

We had almost arrived at Grandma and Grandpa's house when we drove past a garage sale. Mom and Dad loved to look for deals, so we stopped to take a look. Dad found a radio for one dollar that was not working, but he knew it would not be hard to fix it up. When we arrived at Grandma and Grandpa's house, Grandpa was outside working on the upkeep of the front yard.

---

*immaculate impecable.

Questions about the story

1. Why does Grandma and Grandpa's house look immaculate?
2. Who helped Mom make the food before they left?
3. What did mom do while Dad packed the car?
4. What did Stephen do to help get ready for the trip?
5. What did Dad do to make more room in the trunk?
6. When did the family finally leave for Grandpa and Grandma's house?
7. What Did dad buy at the garage sale?
8. What was Grandpa doing when the family arrived to visit?

Questions for discussion

1. Who makes the food In your family?
2. Who does the dishes at your home? Is it fair or unfair? Why or Why not?
3. Do you usually put things back in the correct place after you use them?
4. What are some odds and ends that you might do on the weekend or in your free time?
5. What are some things that you could buy at a garage sale?

Visitando a la familia

El domingo nuestra familia normalmente visitaba a la abuela y el abuelo. La abuela cuidaba la casa muy bien y esta siempre se veía impecable. Normalmente los visitábamos después del desayuno. Papá ayudaba a mamá a prepararlo y todos nos sentábamos a la mesa a disfrutar. Despues del desayuno, ayudábamos a mama a limpiar la cocina mientras papá arreglaba el carro para el viaje.

Ya que era mi turno de lavar platos, inicié con la limpieza rápidamente. Mamá pidió a Stephen que sacara la basura y ayudara a papa a limpiar la cajuela para tener espacio para nuestras cosas. Una vez que todos los platos estaban de vuelta en su lugar y el carro estaba listo con nuestras cosas, nos pusimos en camino.

Estábamos a punto de llegar a la casa de los abuelos cuando pasamos por una venta de garaje. A mamá y papá les encantaban encontrar buenos precios, y nos detuvimos a mirar. Papá encontró un radio que no funcionaba por un dolar, pero sabía que no seria muy difícil arreglarlo. Cuando llegamos a la casa de los abuelos, el abuelo estaba haciendo mantenimiento del jardín.

Chapters ⑥ - ⑩

Review Chapters 6-10 and fill in the crossword below.

Answers ➜ P.172

Across

01. to view items in store window displays without buying
10. a thorough or extensive cleaning of a house
12. Go help your father _____ _____ the garage to make room for your new car.
13. Mr. Jones surprised his students with a _____ quiz every few weeks to keep them on their toes.
14. Robin pulled _____ the driveway to park.
15. The LCD TV that Mia had seen advertized was sold out, so she asked the clerk for a _____ _____.
16. I know you're hungry, but you shouldn't _____ _____ your food.
20. I cooked dinner so it's your job to _____ _____ _____.
22. With the holiday season over, Mia and Cindy were ready to go to the stores and _____ _____ bargains.
23. After eating at the restaurant, Tammy asked for a _____ _____ to take home what she could not finish.
24. On weekends, Fred loves to pig out on _____ _____ while watching TV.
25. No time for lunch… I'll have to _____ _____ _____ between appointments.

Down

02. several small projects that need to be done around the house
03. Make sure you stop to _____ up some milk and bread on your way home.
04. Jill was in such a hurry that she _____ _____ _____ and caused an accident.
05. John, make sure you _____ _____ the garbage before you go out.
06. Jane _____ _____ _____ all weekend to prepare for the test on Monday.
07. It may have only been a _____ _____, but my neck really hurts.
08. Jill was such a _____'__ _____ that none of the other students liked her.
09. David _____ _____ of school to join the circus.
11. Whenever I see a commercial for Pringles, I _____ ____ _____ for potato chips.
17. to drive to the side of the road and stop
18. Einstein lost interest in school and finally _____ out.
19. It's best to _____ _____ on supplies when you live in the wilderness.
21. Driving in _____ and _____ traffic can be quite frustrating.

Special Dates & Events

hold an event
to have an event; to organize and be responsible for an event.
celebrar un evento; organizar y ser responsable por un evento.

La compañía de Dan planificaba hold an event **para conmemorar la fusión de compañías.**
Dan's company planned to hold an event to commemorate the company merger.

take place
to happen; to occur.
ocurrir; darse lugar en.

¿Sabes a qué hora take place **la reunión?**
Do you know what time the meeting is supposed to take place?

go off
to happen in a particular way, usually as planned.
suceder según lo planificado.

Creo que, considerando todo, la promoción de ventas go off **muy bien.**
Well, I think that, all things considered, the marketing promotion for our new product went off well.
* This idiom is mostly used in the past tense.
Normalmente se usa en el tiempo pasado.

be rained out
for an event to be canceled due to rain.
cancelarse un evento por culpa de la lluvia.
* **Noun** rain out.

El evento benéfico para recaudar fondos para las víctimas de la inundación be rained out **ayer.**
The charity event in the city park that planned to raise money for flood victims was rained out yesterday.

fall through
for a plan to fail to happen or occur; for an idea to fail to come about.
fracasar un plan; fracasar una idea; no materializarse un plan.

La joven pareja se emocionó al enterarse de que mientras el financiamiento no fall through, iban a poder tener una casa nueva en los próximos días.

The young couple was excited to learn that as long as the financing didn't fall through, they would own a new house within days.

turn out (for)
to attend or take part in an event.
asistir o tomar parte de un evento.
__Noun__ turnout. Asistencia.

Los planificadores se alegraron al ver que al evento turn out más de cien personas de lo esperado.

Event planners were pleased to see that over one hundred more people turned out for the event than expected.

turn away
to refuse to let someone enter an event.
no permitir que alguien ingrese a un evento.

Los porteros tuvieron que turn away a multitudes de gente en el club el viernes pasado.

Doormen had to turn away hordes of people at the popular nightclub last Friday night.

sellout
an event for which all the tickets are sold.
cuando todos los boletos para un evento están vendidos; no hay boletos disponibles.

Aaron intentó en vano conseguir boletos para el concierto de U2 porque ya estaban sellout.

Aaron tried in vain to get tickets to the popular U2 rock concert, but it was a sellout.

come up
to happen soon.
suceder pronto.

El cumpleaños de Alex come up. ¿Le compraste algún regalo?

Alex's birthday is coming up. Did you get him a gift?

*The progressive and the past tense forms are most commonly used.
Es más común utilizar el progresivo y el tiempo pasado con este modismo.

F ill in the blanks with the appropriate idioms.

01 Friday lunch meetings _____ _____ at a different restaurant each week. Las reuniones del día viernes se llevan acabo en un restaurante diferente cada semana.

02 When it was Stephen's turn to use the company's box seats, the game was _____ _____ .
Cuando le tocó a Stephen utilizar los asientos de la compañía, el partido fue cancelado debido a la lluvia.

03 Connie and her husband knew that their week off was over a month away, but it would _____ up quickly.
Connie y su esposo sabían que faltaba más de un mes para su semana libre, pero sabían que llegaría pronto.

04 With the unexpected success of the new film, ushers had to _____ _____ people at the box office.
Debido al éxito inesperado de la nueva película, los organizadores tuvieron que negar entradas a las personas que se encontraban en la boletería.

05 The surprise birthday party for my dad _____ _____ perfectly.
La fiesta sorpresa de cumpleaños para mi papá se realizó sin problemas.

06 Martin was devastated when financial support for his new restaurant fell _____ at the last minute.
Martin estaba devastado cuando a última hora el apoyo financiero para su nuevo restaurante no se materializó.

07 Amy and Marla were thrilled when they learned their play was _____ _____ .
Amy y Marla estaban muy emocionadas cuando se enteraron de que se habían vendido todos los boletos para su obra.

08 Pete did not expect any professional hockey scouts to _____ _____ for his last game as a university student, so he was surprised when he saw one.
Pete no esperaba que profesionales del equipo de jockey llegaran a ver su último partido como estudiante, por esta razón, se emocionó al verlos.

09 The town mayor decided to _____ a special _____ to honor the memory of Ken Saltmarsh, a talented local artist who gave a great deal back to the community.
El alcalde decidió celebrar un evento especial en honor de la memoria de Ken Saltmarsh, un artista local que siempre aportó mucho a su comunidad.

Read the following story and refer to the questions below.

- Romantic Getaway

One of the biggest decisions that Carrie and Russell had to make this year was to decide where to go to celebrate their tenth anniversary. Since they had been married ten years ago on New Year's Eve, each year they had traveled someplace different to celebrate their anniversary and the New Year. There were always special events being held wherever they went.

Last year's plans fell through because they had not booked their room early enough. January would always come up very quickly. Together they chose to spend the holidays in Vancouver, and celebrate the New Year in a chalet* in Whistler, British Columbia. They knew that the tickets for the party sold out early; the party was going to be one to remember. Carrie had heard from friends that some celebrities would probably turn out for a party or two on New Year's Eve.

They both knew that if word got around that a few celebrities would be attending the parties, every chalet in Whistler would be packed. Resort staff would have to turn away people without reservations for the parties.

Both Carrie and Russell liked the activities that would take place at the ski resort. They hoped that this years' events would go off without a hitch* and that they would have the time of their lives, but being close to Vancouver, the only thing that would dampen* their celebration would be if temperatures were not cold enough and there was a rain out instead of a snowfall.

chalet chalet. *hitch* problema.
dampen humedecer

Questions about the story

1. What happened to last years' plans for Carrie and Russell?

2. What always happened quickly?

3. Where did they enjoy spending their anniversaries?

4. Who might turn out for the party on New Year's Eve?

5. What might happen if there are too many people at the party?

6. Why did Russell like the ski resort?

Questions for discussion

1. Have you ever been turned away from an event or a business? Why?

2. When was the last time that some of your plans fell through?

3. What is the next big holiday that is coming up?
What do you plan to do?

4. Have you ever planned an event?
How did it go off?

5. Name a few sporting events that could be rained out.

6. What is the single most important event that will take place in your life?

Vacaciones románticas

Una de las decisiones mas grandes que Carrie y Russel debían tomar este año era donde iban a celebrar su decimo aniversario. Ya que se casaron hace diez años en la víspera de Año Nuevo, cada año habían viajado a diferentes lugares para celebrar su aniversario y el Año Nuevo. Siempre se daban eventos especiales dondequiera que fueran. Los planes del año pasado fracasaron porque no habían reservado su hotel con tiempo. Enero siempre llegaba muy rapido. Juntos, decidieron pasar las fiestas en Vancouver y celebrar el Año Nuevo en un chalet en Whistler, Columbia Británica. Sabían que los boletos para la fiesta se agotaron rapido, iba a ser una fiesta inolvidable. Carrie había escuchado por algunos amigos que algunas celebridades probablemente llegarían a alguna fiesta en la víspera de Año Nuevo. Ambos sabían que si el resto de la gente se enteraba de que algunas celebridades estarían allí para las fiestas, todas las cabañas en Whistler se llenarían. Los empleados del centro turístico tendrían que negar entrada a las personas sin reservaciones para las fiestas.

Tanto a Carrie como a Russel les interesaban las actividades que se llevarían a cabo en el centro turístico de esqui. Esperaban que este añolos eventos se dieran sin ningún contratiempo y que pudieran a disfrutar al máximo, pero al estar cerca de Vancouver, lo único que podría dañar su celebracion era que la temperatura no fuera lo suficientemente fria y que lloviera, en lugar de nevar.

Telephone Talk ⑫

make a call
to use the telephone to contact someone.
utilizar el teléfono para hacer una llamada.

Kate compró una tarjeta de llamadas para no tener que utilizar monedas cada vez que tenía que make a call.

Kate purchased a phone card so she would not need change each time she wanted to make a call.

*Adjectives such as 'important', 'quick' and 'urgent' are often added to the idiom. A menudo se utiliza adjetivos como 'important' (importante), 'quick' (rápido) y 'urgent' (urgente).

call (someone) up
to call someone; to use the telephone to contact another person.
llamar a alguien; utilizar el teléfono para contactar a otra persona.
*Synonym give someone a call.

Necesito call Tom up y preguntarle a qué hora tenemos que encontrarnos en el centro comercial.

I need to call Tom up and ask him what time we are supposed to meet at the mall.

on the phone
to be using the telephone; to be in the middle of a phone call.
utilizar el teléfono; realizar una llamada.
*Synonym on the line. En línea.

Dwayne preguntó a su hermana cuánto tiempo iba a on the phone.

Dwayne asked his older sister how long she would be on the phone.

off the phone
not to be using the telephone.
colgar el teléfono.

"Cariño, avísame cuando hayas off the phone. Necesito hacer una llamada."

"Hey honey, let me know when you are off the phone. I need to make a call."

hold on

to tell someone to wait.

decirle a alguien que espere.

Synonym put on hold.

Celia pidió al empleado del hotel que hold on **mientras buscaba una pluma y un papel para escribir la información de la reservación.**

Celia asked the hotel clerk to hold on while she grabbed a pen and paper to write down the reservation information.

hang up

to end a phone call by placing the handset correctly on the base unit.

terminar una llamada colgando el teléfono.

Ya que su llamada no pasó, Tina decidió hang up **e intentar más tarde.**

Since her call would not go through, Tina decided to hang up and try again later.

get cut off

for a phone call to end abruptly due to technical problems.

cuando una llamada telefónica termina bruscamente por problemas técnicos.

Cuando Mark llama a sus papás desde otro país, get cut off **por una mala conexión.**

Every time Mark calls his parents from overseas, he ends up getting cut off because of a bad connection.

hang up on someone

to end a call abruptly with out saying good-bye, usually done in anger.

terminar una llamada sin despedirse, normalmente cuando uno está enojado. España: cerrar el teléfono.

Cuando la mamá de Tom le dijo que no podía quedarse más tarde, Tom hang up on her **bruscamente.**

When Tom's mother told him he could not stay out later, Tom abruptly hung up on her.

off the hook

for the telephone to be incorrectly placed on its base, disabling the telephone.

cuando el teléfono está descolgado.

El teléfono estaba off the hook **por error, por eso Cindy no podía llamar a sus papás.**

The phone was accidentally left off the hook, so Cindy could not get through to her parents.

on the hook

for the telephone to be correctly on its base, making it able to receive calls.

colgar el teléfono correctamente para poder recibir llamadas.

Dalton se aseguró en poner el teléfono on the hook **cuando terminó su llamada.**

Dalton made sure to put the phone back on the hook when he was done making his call.

call someone back
to return someone's call; to phone someone that called and was unable to reach you.
devolver la llamada a alguien.

make a prank call
to make an annoying or mischievous 'joke' call to someone.
hacer una llamada de broma.
*__Synonym__ crank call.

over the phone
by way of the telephone.
vía telefónica; por teléfono.

Necesito call back **a Dan. Él me llamó de mañana cuando estaba fuera de la oficina.**
need to call Dan back. He called me earlier this morning when I was out of the office.

Los estudiantes encontraron el número de teléfono de la profesora y decidieron make a prank call **a media noche.**
The students found out their teacher's phone number and decided to make a prank call to her in the middle of the night.

Ali no quiso dar su información financiera over the phone **al vendedor por razones de seguridad.**
Ali did not want to give his financial information to the sales person over the phone for security reasons.

Fill in the blanks with the appropriate idioms.

01 Chris put the phone back on _____ _____ once he realized it had been knocked off.

Chris puso el teléfono en su lugar cuando se dio cuenta de que estaba descolgado.

02 After the busy day at the office, Heather took the phone _____ the _____ so she could rest.

Después de un día muy ajetreado en la oficina, Heather descolgó el teléfono para poder descansar.

03 Since it was his third long distance call of the morning, Winston was hoping not to get _____ _____ before he put in his company's order.

Ya que era su tercera llamada de larga distancia de la mañana, Winston esperaba que la llamada no se cortara antes de poder hacer la orden de la compañía.

04 As soon as Charles got through to the restaurant, the hostess asked him to _____ _____ while she took a call.

Tan pronto Charles logró contactarse con el restaurante, la mesera le pidió que esperara mientras recibía otra llamada.

05 As soon as Jared arrived home from work, he decided to _____ _____ some friends and make plans for the evening.

Tan pronto Jared llegó a casa del trabajo, decidió llamar a algunos amigos y hacer planes para la noche.

06 Arnold saved time by doing his banking _____ _____ _____ instead of going to the bank.

Arnold ahorró tiempo arreglando sus cuentas bancarias por teléfono en vez de ir al banco.

07 On school nights, Riana had to be _____ _____ _____ by 10:00 o'clock.

Las noches anteriores a ir a clases, Riana tenía que colgar el teléfono antes de las 10 de la noche.

08 Dad was waiting for an important call so he asked that no one be _____ _____ _____ between 5:00 and 7:00 in the evening.

Papá esperaba una llamada importante, así que pidió que nadie utilizara el teléfono desde las 5 hasta las 7 de la noche.

09 The babysitter thought the children were asleep, but they were actually using the telephone to _____ _____ _____ by dialing numbers at random.

La niñera pensaba que los niños estaban dormidos, pero lo que estaban haciendo era utilizar el teléfono para hacer bromas marcando números al azar.

10 After a lengthy argument, Sunny chose to _____ _____ on her boyfriend.

Después de una pelea larga, Sunny decidió colgarle el teléfono a su novio.

11 Once James realized he was speaking with a salesperson, he immediately chose to _____ _____ the phone.

Una vez que James se dio cuenta de que estaba hablando con una vendedora, decidió colgar el teléfono inmediatamente.

12 The message said that Lisa should _____ the doctor's office _____ to reschedule her appointment.

El mensaje decía que Lisa tenía que devolver la llamada al consultorio del doctor para cambiar su cita.

13 After looking at the newspaper advertisements, Tim decided to make _____ _____ to see just how much the item would cost.

Después de mirar los anuncios del periódico, Tim decidió hacer una llamada para averiguar el costo del artículo.

Answers 1. (on) the hook 2. off (the) hook 3. (get) cut off 4. hold on 5. call up 6. over the phone 7. off the phone 8. on the phone 9. make prank calls 10. hang up (on her boyfriend) 11. hang up 12. call (the doctor's office) back 13. (make) a call

Read the following story and refer to the questions below.

- Harp Strings and Phone Things

Cleo was hired to work as a promotional salesman for a small company that specialized in selling premium harp strings. Working for a young company was quite challenging, so he knew he would be on the phone for hours at a time.

After training on the telephone system, he had to make calls to every music store in the country. Cleo had to manage five telephones and make sure not to get cut off or accidentally hang up on any potential customers. The most important calls were those when a customer would call back to order more harp strings. He would get their information over the phone, quickly take their order, and try to get off the phone as soon as possible to save time. Sometimes he would be so busy that he would have to ask customers to hold on while he answered another line. With all of the calls coming in and going out, it was not hard to mistakenly leave one phone off the hook.

Selling harp strings over the phone was not as easy as Cleo thought it would be. Some stores actually thought he was making prank calls when he began his sales pitch* and hung up on him. The last thing he thought he would be doing for a living was calling up people and asking them to buy harp strings.

---

*sales pitch argumento de ventas.

Questions about the story

1. What is the main character's job?
2. What is he required to do every day?
3. What does he have to make sure does not happen?
4. What calls were considered to be the most important?
5. Why would he ask customers to hold on?
6. What kinds of mistakes do you think that he often made?
7. Did Cleo ever make prank calls?
8. Did he ever think that he would be calling up strangers for a living?

Questions for discussion

1. On average, how many phone calls do you make a day?
2. How long are you on the phone each day?
3. Have you ever hung up on someone? Why?
4. Have you ever been hung up on? Why?
5. When you were younger, did you ever make prank calls?
6. What is the longest that you are willing to wait on hold before you hang up?
7. Do you talk to telemarketers or do you just hang up them? Why or why not?

Cosas de teléfono y cuerdas de arpa

Cleo fue contratado para trabajar como vendedor para una compañía pequeña especializada en la venta de cuerdas de arpa. El trabajar para una compañía joven era algo muy exigente, así que sabia que iba a pasar largas horas en el teléfono.

Después de recibir entrenamiento en el sistema telefónico, tuvo que llamar a todas las tiendas de música en el pais. Cleo tenía que trabajar con cinco teléfonos a la vez y asegurarse de no perder llamadas o colgar el teléfono por accidente mientras hablaba con un posible cliente. Las llamadas más importantes eran aquellas en las que el cliente devolvia la llamada para hacer otro pedido de cuerdas de arpa. Él debía recopilar informacion por teléfono, tomar el pedido rápidamente, y terminar la llamada lo más pronto posible para ahorrar tiempo. A veces estaba tan ocupado que debía pedirles a los clientes que esperaran mientras el contestaba otra linea. Con todas las llamadas entrantes y salientes era difícil no dejar un teléfono descolgado por error.

Making Conversation

make small talk
to discuss relatively unimportant topics or issues; to make idle conversation.
hablar sobre temas inconsecuentes; hablar banalidades.

Cuando se fue la luz, la gente en el ascensor make small talk **para pasar el tiempo.**
When the electricity went out, the people in the elevator chose to make small talk to pass the time.

shoot the breeze
to talk or chat informally with no real objective.
hablar por hablar.
Synonym shoot the shit. (very informal slang, used only between good friends).
(Modismo muy informal; utilizado solamente entre muy buenos amigos.)

Durante el descanso al medio tiempo del partido de fútbol, Jim shoot the breeze **con sus amigos.**
During half time at the soccer game, Jim shoots the breeze with his friends.

break the ice
to make a person whom you have not met before feel more relaxed by initiating discussion.
romper el hielo; hacer que una persona desconocida se sienta más relajada al empezar una conversación
Synonym ice-breaker

Tom contó un chiste para break the ice **con los papás de su novia.**
Tom used a funny joke to break the ice with his girlfriend's parents.
*a game or joke that makes people who do not know each other feel more relaxed together.
Un juego o chiste que ayuda a un grupo de personas que no se conocen a sentirse más cómodos. Romper el silencio.

strike up a conversation
to start a conversation with someone for the first time.

Ya que la alumna nueva era muy bonita, Joshua decidió strike up a

iniciar una conversación con alguien por primera vez.

conversation **con ella durante el almuerzo.**

The new girl at school was very attractive, so Joshua decided to strike up a conversation with her during their lunch hour.

shake hands
to greet another person by grasping their hand and shaking it.
saludar a otra persona apretando su mano y moviéndola.

El primer día en su nueva oficina, Greg se aseguró de shake hands **a todos sus nuevos colegas.**

On his first day at his new office, Greg made sure to shake hands with all of his new colleagues.

a sight for sore eyes
an object or person that one is delighted to see again; a welcome sight.
cuando estás feliz de ver a alguien o algo; un deleite para los ojos. Comúnmente se dice 'dichosos los ojos que te ven'.

Los niños habían estado caminando muchas cuadras, así que cuando vieron a su mamá, ella fue a sight for sore eyes**.**

The boys had been walking for many blocks, so when they saw their mom, she was a sight for sore eyes.

*In this expression, the speaker is saying that seeing the subject brings about a forgotten sense of enjoyment or happiness.
En esta frase, la persona intenta decir que ver a la persona causa un sentido olvidado de alegría o felicidad.

have not seen someone for ages
to have not met or greeted a person for a long time.
no haber visto a alguien por años.

Sally have not seen **sus amigas de la universidad** her college friends for ages **por eso casi no las reconoció en la reunión.**

Sally hadn't seen her college friends for ages so she hardly recognized them at the reunion.

have not seen someone in a dog's age
to say that it has been a long time since you have seen someone.
comentar que ha pasado mucho tiempo desde que se vio a alguien.

"have not seen you in a dog's age**," dijo Sandra a Tom cuando se encontraron en la fiesta.**

"I haven't seen you in a dog's age," Sandra said to Tom when they bumped into each other at the party.

*The term dog's age is used because dogs age faster than humans so it usually implies a large number of years.
El término 'dog's age' se utiliza porque los perros envejecen mas rápido que las personas; es decir que implica muchos años.

long time no see

to express that a long period of time has passed since two people have met.

expresar que ha pasado mucho tiempo desde que se han visto.

España: Tanto tiempo sin verte.

"long time no see," le dijo David a su primo cuando se encontraron donde siempre pasan vacaciones.

"Long time no see," David said to his cousin as they met at their annual vacation spot.

*This idiom is informal and is usually used between close friends.
Este modismo es informal y normalmente se utiliza entre amigos cercanos.

what's up?

a casual way to ask someone how they are.

¿qué tal?; ¿qué hay?; manera casual de preguntar a alguien como está.

*Synonym what's new?; what's happening?; what's going on?; what's shakin'?

Al entrar al bar, Chris gritó "what's up?" al barman y sus amigos.

As Chris entered the bar he shouted, "What's up?" to the bartender and his friends.

*All of the above idioms are used in every day conversation. Common responses to the question are: 'Nothing', 'Not much', 'Nothing special', etc.
Todos los modismos anteriores son utilizados cotidianamente. Algunas respuestas comunes son: 'nothing' (nada), 'not much' (nada interesante), 'nothing special' (nada en especial), etc.

catch someone later

to say good-bye with the expectation that you will meet again in the near future.

despedir con la esperanza de encontrarse otra vez en un futuro cercano.

Después de la reunión del equipo, Jake dijo, "catch you later."

After the team meeting, Jake said, "I'll catch you later."

see you around

to say good-bye informally.

despedirse informalmente; nos vemos. España: nos vemos por allí.

James dijo a Mike, "see you around," cuando se despidieron después de la escuela.

James said, "See you around," to Mike as they parted after school.

take care

to say goodbye and wish someone to be cautious and stay well.

despedirse y desear que alguien se cuide.

Cuando estaban saliendo, la abuela les dijo que take care en el viaje largo a casa.

As they were leaving, Grandma told them to take care on the long drive home.

F ill in the blanks with the appropriate idioms.

01 When Ian and Ray ran into each other at the grocery store, they _____ small _____ for a few minutes.

Cuando Ian y Ray se encontraron en el supermercado, ellos hablaron banalidades por unos momentos.

02 "_____ _____ no _____," said Hannah as she entered the dance studio for the first time in months.

"¡Hace mucho tiempo que no te veo!", dijo Hannah cuando entró al estudio de danza por primera vez en meses.

03 Teachers usually plan to have the students participate in fun activities to _____ the _____ during the first week of school.

Los profesores normalmente planifican hacer que los estudiantes participen en actividades divertidas para romper el hielo en la primera semana de clases.

04 Ali was very outgoing, so it was never a problem for him to _____ up _____ conversation with someone he just met.

Ali era muy sociable, por esta razón nunca tuvo problema para iniciar una conversación con alguien que acababa de conocer.

05 Since they lived so far away and were always working, the old friends had not _____ _____ _____ for _____.

Ya que vivían tan lejos y siempre estaban trabajando, los viejos amigos no se habían visto en años.

06 In North America, it is customary to _____ _____ with people that you are introduced to.

En América del Norte, es costumbre apretar la mano de la gente cuando uno es presentado.

07 Sometimes, Anthony would _____ the _____ with his neighbor over the fence.

A veces, a Anthony le gustaba charlar por encima de la cerca con su vecino.

08 Aunt Bernice always yelled for us to _____ _____ as we pulled out of the driveway.

La tía Bernice siempre nos decía a gritos que nos cuidemos mientras salíamos de su entrada.

09 When the coach came out at the end of practice with water for everyone, it was a _____ _____ _____ _____.

Cuando el entrenador salió al final de la practica con agua para todos, eran dichosos los ojos que lo veían.

10 Tim yelled "_____'_____ _____?" as he entered the room full of people.

Tim grito "¿qué tal?", cuando entró a la habitación llena de gente.

11 Sarah hollered, "I'll _____ you _____," over her shoulder to her friends as she left the coffee shop in a hurry.

Sara gritó, "Nos vemos después", a sus amigas cuando salió corriendo del café.

12 After the argument with her boyfriend, Lara said, "_____ _____ around," and walked out the door.

Después de la pelea con su novio, Lara dijo, "Nos vemos", y salió por la puerta.

13 Ian had not seen his friend Mustapha _____ _____ dog's _____ so he hardly recognized him when they met on the street.

Ian no había visto a su amigo Mustapha por mucho tiempo, por esta razón casi no lo reconoció cuando lo vio en la calle.

Answers 1. made (small) talk 2. Long time (no) see 3. break (the) ice 4. strike (up) a (conversation) 5. (had not) seen each other (for) ages 6. shake hands 7. shoot (the) breeze 8. take care 9. (a) sight for sore eyes 10. What's up 11. catch (you) later 12. see you (around) 13. (seen his friend Mustapha) in a (dog's) age

Read the following story and refer to the questions below.

- A Hard Night's Networking

Barry stepped onto the train that was to take him to the annual conference for all of the top salespeople in the company. He struck up a conversation with the person next to him. It didn't take long for him to realize that his new acquaintance* would be attending the conference too. When they arrived at their stop, Barry said, "I'll see you around the hotel over the weekend." and his new friend responded, "Sure, I'll catch you later."

Friday, right after supper, Barry participated in a few activities to break the ice, since he had not seen some of his colleagues for ages. Following the icebreaker activities, Barry and a few other company people went down to the bar to shoot the breeze. As more people arrived down at the bar, he tried to get acquainted with as many new people as he could, and decided to shake hands with everyone that came through the door. "Long time no see," said one of Barry's old friends from college as he greeted him with a smile. Barry had not seen Drew in a dog's age. He was a sight for sore eyes. It was nice to finally chat with someone that he already knew. When it got late, Barry told Drew to take care and went up to his room to get some sleep. He had a busy day of meetings the next day.

As he got on the elevator, he heard a man say, "What's up?" It was his friend from the train, who he now realized was the top salesman of the year. "Congratulations on your award! But watch out... I'll be winning next time."

---

*acquaintance conocido.

Questions about the story

1. What did Barry do with the person next to him on the train?
2. What did he say to his new acquaintance?
3. How did Barry break the ice with his business colleagues that he had not seen for ages?
4. When he and his colleagues shoot the breeze, what might they talk about?
5. How did his old college friend greet him?
6. Who hasn't Barry seen in a dog's age?
7. How did his new friend address him in the elevator?

Questions for discussion

1. Do you ever strike up conversations with total strangers? Why? Why not?
2. What might be a good thing to say to break the ice with a stranger?
3. If you were away from home for a month and returned, what would be a sight for sore eyes?
4. Who do you know that is good at making small talk? Why is this person so good?
5. Is there someone that you haven't seen in a dog's age? Who? And where are they now?

Una noche difícil para hacer contactos

Barry subió al tren que lo iba a llevar a la conferencia dirigida a los mejores vendedores de la compañía e inició una conversación con la persona de al lado. No pasó mucho tiempo para que se diera cuenta de que su nuevo amigo también iba a la conferencia. Cuando llegaron a la parada, Barry dijo "Te veré en el hotel este fin de semana". Y su nuevo amigo le dijo, "Claro, nos veremos luego".

El día viernes, después de la cena, Barry participó en algunas actividades para romper el hielo porque no había visto a algunos de sus colegas en mucho tiempo. Después de las actividades para "romper el hielo", Barry y algunas personas de la compañía fueron al bar para conversar. Mientras llegaba más gente al bar, Barry intentaba hacerse conocer por todas las personas y decidió dar la mano a todos los que entraban por la puerta. "Hace mucho tiempo que no te veo", le dijo un viejo amigo universitario. Barry no había visto a Drew en mucho tiempo. "Dichosos los ojos que te ven", pensó. Se sintió muy bien de hablar con alguien que ya conocía. Cuando se hizo tarde, Barry le dijo a Drew que se cuidase y se fue a su habitación a dormir pues tenía muchas reuniones el próximo día.

Cuando entraba al ascensor, escuchó a alguien decir "¿qué tal?". Se trataba de su amigo del tren, el mejor vendedor del año, algo de lo que Barry recién se había dado cuenta. "Felicitaciones por tu premio. Pero ten cuidado, yo seré quien gane la próxima vez".

He Said, She Said  14

(a) penny for your thoughts
a way to ask someone to speak their mind.
¿en qué piensas?; forma de pedirle a otra persona que diga lo que piensa.

Sé cuando estás con mucho estrés…, a penny for your thoughts.
I can tell when you're stressed – a penny for your thoughts.

hold it down
to politely request that someone lower the volume of their conversation.
pedirle a alguien que baje el volumen.

Oye, estoy estudiando, ¿puedes hold it down por favor?
Hey guys, I'm trying to study so could you hold it down please?
In this idiom 'it' is often replaced by 'the noise'.
A veces, en vez de decir, 'it', se dice 'the noise' (ruido).

fire away
to begin asking questions; to question or speak freely.
comenzar a hacer preguntas; hacer preguntas o hablar con libertad.

El presidente dio paso a las preguntas diciendo, "fire away."
The president opened the floor to questions saying, "Fire away".

speak one's mind
to say exactly what one thinks or wants to say.
decir lo que se piensa.

Si la quieres, debes speak your mind antes de que encuentre otro.
If you love her, you'd better speak your mind before she finds someone else.
Usually after waiting to say something for a long time.
Normalmente utilizado después de haber esperado mucho tiempo para decir algo.

clam up
to suddenly stop talking and refuse to say any more; to choose not to talk or respond.
dejar de hablar; no hablar más; callarse.

Mi esposa clam up **cuando hablo de tener más hijos.**
My wife just clams up whenever I mention having more children.

off the top of one's head
one's first thought; spontaneously, without time for thought, research or verification.
lo primero que se viene a la mente; improvisadamente, sin tiempo para pensar, investigar o verificar.
Synonym off the cuff.

off the top of **my** head**, diría que él estaba conduciendo a altas velocidades, pero no estoy seguro.**
Off the top of my head, I'd say that he was speeding, but I'm not certain.

blurt out
to speak suddenly without thinking or holding back; to speak impulsively.
soplar; dejar escapar un secreto; decir de repente; decir a boca de jarro.

Por favor, no blurt out **las respuestas ya que este es un examen escrito.**
Please do not blurt out the answers as this is a written test.

have a way with words
to express oneself well.
expresarse muy bien; tener facilidad de palabra.
Synonym have the gift of gab.

Como poeta y estadista, él have a way with words **y hace que la gente lo escuche.**
As a poet and statesman, he had a way with words that made people listen.

beat around the bush
to evade the issue, hint or stall without coming to the point; to fail to address a subject or topic directly.
evadir el tema; irse por las ramas.

Deja de beat around the bush**, y llega al punto.**
Stop beating around the bush and just get to the point.

get one's message across
to get someone to understand; to convey one's thoughts clearly.
hacer entender; dar a comprender el mensaje.

Aunque los niños no hablaban inglés creo que get my message across**.**
Even though the kids didn't speak English, I think I got my message across to them.

cat got your tongue
a question when someone is unable to speak, meaning: why don't you say something?
¿te comió la lengua el ratón?; pregunta para alguien que no habla.
Synonym has the cat got your tongue?

¿Qué pasó? cat got your tongue **¿Por qué llegas tan tarde?**
What's the matter? Cat got your tongue? Why are you so late?

F ill in the blanks with the appropriate idioms.

01 You hate me!! Don't _____ around the _____ Barbara, and tell me what you really think!
¡Me odias! Deja de evadir el tema Bárbara, ¡dime lo que en verdad piensas!

02 You've been brooding over that book all day. A _____ for your _____.
Has estado meditando en ese libro todo el día, ¿en qué piensas?

03 John is almost too willing to _____ his _____. Most of us just wish he'd keep it to himself.
John siempre está dispuesto a decir lo que piensa. Nosotros preferiríamos que no lo dijese.

04 The Senator from Massachusetts tried to _____ _____ _____ _____ that he would not accept corruption in the government.
El Senador de Massachusetts quiso que todos comprendieran que no va a aceptar corrupción en su gobierno.

05 Reporters _____ _____ at the head of the oil conglomerate during a press conference.
Los reporteros hicieron sus preguntas a los gerentes de la compañía petrolera durante la rueda de prensa.

06 Whenever Jerry would get excited, he'd _____ _____ comments that sometimes seemed rude to the others that were near him.
Cuando Jerry se emocionaba, hacía comentarios que resultaban ser groseros para otras personas.

07 Unprepared for the meeting, the presenter had to answer the questions _____ the _____ of his _____.
Como no estaba preparado para la reunión, el presentador tuvo que responder las preguntas con lo primero que se le vino a la mente.

08 Frank is one of those people who just _____ a way _____ _____. He always has an interesting point of view that people want to listen to.
Frank es un tipo que utiliza bien las palabras. Siempre tiene un punto de vista muy interesante que captura la atención de la gente.

09 When they were arrested, the illegal immigrants _____ _____ and pretended not to understand English.
Los inmigrantes ilegales se callaron cuando fueron arrestados y fingieron no entender inglés.

10 The neighbors upstairs were always asking us to _____ the noise _____ even though we were being rather quiet.
Los vecinos de arriba siempre nos pedían que bajáramos el volumen aunque no hiciéramos mucho ruido.

11 I asked you a simple question. Why don't you just answer me? _____

_____ _____ _____?

Te hice una pregunta simple. ¿Por qué no me contestas? ¿Te comió la lengua el ratón?

Read the following story and refer to the questions below.

- China Talk

As the tour bus pulled into the parking lot near the Great Wall of China, the guide, who had a way with words, described the sights they were going to see. It sounded as if he was speaking off the top of his head, yet his language had been well rehearsed. He got his message across and then opened up the floor* for questions. "Fire away," he said.

A couple of people asked common questions and then a tall, quiet man named Dan started to speak. He beat around the bush for a while and then, just as he seemed to be getting to the point, he clammed up. Everyone listened intently,* but he said nothing. Then the guide said jokingly, "Penny for your thoughts…" as one of the women hushed him saying, "Shhh." And still Dan said nothing, struggling for the words to come out.

Finally, a less patient man shouted, "What? Cat got your tongue? Just blurt it out man!" After a long pause, the tall, quiet man spoke, "Is it OK, I mean, for us to speak our minds? With this being a communist country and all… will they arrest us for talking about our ideals?" Everyone on the bus roared in laughter. "OK, hold it down everyone," the guide said to calm them down as he spoke softly to reassure Dan. "Don't worry Dan, you'll be fine."

---

*intently atentamente *open the floor dar paso a

Questions about the story

1. How did the tour guide speak?
   Did he have a way with words?
2. What did he say after he got his message across? Why?
3. How did Dan speak at first?
   What did he do before getting to the point?
4. What did the guide say to stimulate him?
5. How did the woman hush the guide?
6. What happened when a man got impatient?
7. What was Dan's concern in the end?
8. Why did the people laugh? Were Dan's fears real?

Questions for discussion

1. In your society, is it considered acceptable to speak your mind in public?
2. How would you respond if I offered you a penny for your thoughts right now?
3. Do you beat around the bush when you have something difficult to say?
4. Tell me about a time you or someone else clammed up.
5. Have you ever met someone that had a way with words?
   Describe him or her.

Conversaciones en China

Cuando el bus de turismo ingresó al estacionamiento cerca de la Gran Muralla China, el guía, quien era bueno con las palabras, describió lo que verían. Parecía que decía lo primero que le venía a la mente, pero su lenguaje era muy bueno. Comprendimos lo que estaba diciendo y luego dio paso a las preguntas diciendo: "¡hagan sus preguntas!" Algunas personas hicieron preguntas normales pero después, un hombre alto y tímido llamado Dan, empezó a hablar. Durante un rato se fue por las ramas y cuando por fin parecía que iba al grano, se calló. Todos escucharon atentamente, pero no dijo nada. Entonces el guía bromeando dijo, "¡dígame lo que piensa!" mientras una de las señoras lo callaba diciendo, "Shh". Aun así Dan no dijo nada, seguía intentando sacar palabras. Al final, un hombre con poca paciencia gritó, "¿qué? ¿te comió la lengua el ratón? ¡Simplemente habla!" Después de una pausa larga, el hombre habló, "¿No hay problema en decir lo que se nos viene a la mente? Como este es un país comunista... ¿no nos arrestarán si hablamos sobre nuestros ideales?" Toda la gente en el bus empezo a reír. "OK, bajen el volumen todos", dijo el guía para calmarles mientras hablaba despacio para tranquilizar a Dan. "No te preocupes Dan, no vas a tener problemas."

Fact or Opinion

for a fact
for certain; without a doubt.
con toda seguridad; sin dudas.

¿Qué pasó con ella? ¿Está acusada de asesinato? ¿Sabes esto for a fact?

She what? She's been accused of murder? Do you know this for a fact?

hear of
to learn of or know about from some report.
darse cuenta o escuchar por medio de algún reporte.

Estoy segura de que hear of los "Irises" de Van Gogh, ¿pero los has visto de cerca?

I'm sure you've heard of Van Gogh's "Irises," but have you ever seen it up close?

*Usually used in the present perfect or past perfect tense.
Normalmente se utiliza en el presente perfecto o el pasado perfecto.

know-how
the practical ability; skill and knowledge needed to do something.
conocimiento práctico; conocimiento para poder hacer algo.

Estamos dispuestos a darte el know-how para poder realizar el trabajo.

We are ready to provide you with the know-how to get the job done.

broaden one's horizons
to branch out and expand one's interests, knowledge, activities and more.
ampliar el conocimiento, intereses y actividades de alguien; ampliar horizontes.

No vine a la universidad para recibir entrenamiento para el trabajo. Vine a broaden my horizons.

I didn't come to college to get job training. I came to broaden my horizons.

pick up
to learn something gradually, quickly or easily.
captar algo lenta, rápida o fácilmente.

Ted pudo pick up **las reglas básicas de ajedrez muy fácilmente cuando era niño.**
Ted was able to pick up the basics of chess easily as a boy.

be news to someone
to learn of something surprising for the first time.
enterarse de algo sorprendente por primera vez.

Todos están hablando sobre la fusión como si yo supiera algo, pero be news to me.
Everyone is talking about the merger as if I should know, but it's news to me.

through the grapevine
by word of mouth; indirectly; through other people.
escuchar por ahí; indirectamente, a través de otras personas. España: me lo ha dicho un pajarito.

Las noticias pasan through the grapevine **más rápido que por fuentes tradicionales.**
News often spreads through the grapevine faster than through traditional news sources.
* This idiom is often used for rumors.
Este modismo a menudo se utiliza cuando corre un rumor.

make of
to come to a logical understanding; to interpret, discern or perceive.
llegar a un entendimiento lógico; percibir, sacar conclusiones.

¿Qué make of **estas marcas en el artefacto?**
What do you make of these markings on this artifact?
*Often used in question form.
A menudo utilizado en forma de pregunta.

get wind of
to hear tell of; to hear rumor of.
enterarse de algo.

La policía acaba de get wind of **de planes para poder apoderarse de la oficina del alcalde.**
The local police just got wind of some plans to take over the mayor's office.
* Usually something secret.
Normalmente algo secreto.

in the know
well informed; aware of things that most people don't know.
ser experto en algo; saber cosas que mucha gente no sabe.

El gerente siempre estaba in the know **sobre las vidas personales de sus trabajadores.**
The manager made it a point to always be in the know about his workers' lives.

in the loop
involved in and informed about; able to make decisions about.
mantenerse informado; capaz de hacer decisiones sobre.
*__Antonym__ out of the loop.

Hasta cuando estoy de vacaciones, quiero mantenerme in the loop **de todas las decisiones hechas.**
Even when I'm on vacation, I want to be kept in the loop on all decisions made.

Fill in the blanks with the appropriate idioms.

01 Have you _____ _____ Tom's death? It was in the obituary last week.

¿Escuchaste de la muerte de Tom? Estaba en el obituario del periódico la semana pasada.

02 My ex-wife is getting married again? That's _____ to _____!
Why didn't you tell me?

¿Se casa otra vez mi ex-esposa? No lo sabía. ¿Por qué no me dijiste?

03 We can rebuild him. We have the technology and the _____-_____ to make him stronger, faster and better than before.

Lo podemos reconstruir. Tenemos la tecnología y el conocimiento para hacerlo más fuerte, más rápido y mejor que antes.

04 Join the army and we'll not only show you the world, we'll _____ your _____.

Enlístate en el ejército y te mostraremos no solamente el mundo, sino también ampliaremos tus horizontes.

05 When the native islanders weren't kept _____ the _____ on foreign policy decisions, they quickly revolted.

Cuando los nativos de la isla no fueron mantenidos al tanto sobre las decisiones de política extranjera, prontamente se rebelaron.

06 Korean and Chinese are some of the hardest languages for foreigners to _____ _____.

El coreano y el chino están entre los idiomas más difíciles para que los extranjeros aprendan.

07 Don't believe everything you hear through _____ _____, but tell me anyway.

No creas todo lo que escuches por ahí, pero cuéntamelo de todas formas.

08 Many people believe the assassination of Kennedy was part of a conspiracy, but no one knows it _____ a _____.

Mucha gente cree que el asesinato de Kennedy fue parte de un complot, pero nadie lo sabe con seguridad.

09 The foreman _____ _____ of some upcoming layoffs, so he started looking for a backup job.

El capataz se enteró de los próximos despidos, así que empezó a buscar otro trabajo.

10 Hey Frank, if you're not _____ the _____, don't try to get involved.

Oye Frank, si no eres un experto, no te involucres.

11 I don't know what to _____ _____ all these UFO sightings and crop designs, but I think they're all a hoax.

No sé qué opinión tener sobre las apariciones de los OVNIS y los diseños en los campos de trigo, pero creo que todo es una broma.

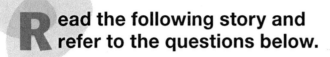

Read the following story and refer to the questions below.

- Dreams, Destinations and Destiny

When Val decided to go backpacking through Europe, it was with the idea of broadening his horizons. He'd heard of people who went and had many interesting experiences. He had hoped to pick up some German, but actually picked up a bit of French instead. After taking trains to a few cities, he developed the know-how to find accommodation* and explore the city.

By talking to other backpackers, he'd get wind of upcoming festivals and the best places to go. At first, he didn't know what to make of the different cultures, but after a couple of months, he knew for a fact that this was the experience he was looking for. He resolved to come back again in the future.

Even though he sent postcards home, they took so long to get there that his mother felt like she was out of the loop. So when he finally came home and called her from the airport, it was news to her. Even though she was happy to see him, she chastised* him for not keeping her in the know. "I don't want to hear about you through the grapevine!" she exclaimed. "Just pick up the phone and call me!"

---

*accommodation alojamiento *chastise reprender

Questions about the story

1. Why did Val decide to go backpacking in Europe?
2. What had he heard about travel from other people?
3. Was he able to pick up any languages?
4. How did he develop the know-how to find accommodation?
5. How did he get wind of upcoming festivals?
6. Was this the experience he was looking for?
7. What did his mother feel like? What was news to her?
8. How did she chastise him? What did she say?

Questions for discussion

1. What would you do if you got wind of interesting information before everyone else?
2. What can you do to broaden your horizons?
3. How would you keep someone out of the loop in order to surprise them?
4. What kind of things do you hear about through the grapevine?
5. Have you been able to pick up any idioms from this lesson?
   Which ones have you already heard of?
   Which ones are news to you?

Sueños, destinos y el destino

Cuando Val decidió mochilear por toda Europa, fue con la intención de ampliar sus horizontes. Había escuchado de personas quienes habían realizado este viaje y habían tenido varias experiencias muy interesantes. Esperaba aprender un poco de alemán, pero terminó aprendiendo un poco de francés. Después de viajar por tren a diferentes ciudades, adquirió conocimientos para encontrar hospedaje y explorar la ciudad.

Al hablar con otros viajeros, se enteraba de los próximos festivales y los mejores lugares para visitar. Al principio, no sabía qué pensar de otras culturas, pero después de algunos meses, sabía definitivamente que esta era la experiencia que buscaba. Resolvió regresar en un futuro próximo.

Aunque mandaba postales a casa, tomaron tanto tiempo en llegar que su mamá sentía que no estaba al tanto de la situación. Entonces cuando por fin llegó y la llamó desde el aeropuerto, fueron grandes noticias para ella. Aunque estaba feliz de verlo, lo regañó por no mantenerla al tanto de su viaje. "¡No quiero enterarme de ti por ahí!" dijo ella, "¡Simplemente encuentra un teléfono y llámame!"

Chapters ⑪ - ⑮

Review Chapters 11-15 and fill in the crossword below.

Answers → P.172

Across

03. Don't believe everything you hear through _____ _____.

05. The new girl tried to _____ _____ a conversation with the football player in the hall.

06. The gifted student was able to _____ _____ the basics of nuclear physics quickly.

10. As soon as you are _____ the phone, let me know. I need to make a call."

11. If you have to talk in front of a group of people, a joke can help to _____ _____ _____.

14. The young couple just wanted their wedding to _____ _____ without a hitch.

15. After the busy day at the office, Heather took the phone off _____ _____ so she could rest.

17. The village decided to _____ _____ event every year in honor of the people who lost their lives in the tsunami.

19. Last year, their trip to Mexico _____ _____ because John broke his leg.

20. Carrie had heard from friends that some celebrities would probably _____ _____ for a party or two on New Year's Eve.

21. When the old friends saw each other, they made _____ _____ for a few minutes.

22. If you don't speak _____ _____, no one will know what you really want.

Down

01. Don't beat _____ _____ _____. Tell me what you really think!

02. The young mother got her _____ across to look both ways before crossing the street.

03. Will the meeting _____ _____, even if the boss doesn't come back in time?

04. Lance spent a summer traveling through Africa to _____ his horizons.

07. The kids loved to make _____ _____ by dialing random numbers and telling jokes.

08. My teenage daughter is _____ _____ _____ for hours at a time with her friends.

09. What's the matter? Cat got _____ _____?

11. The children would _____ _____ the answers to the teacher's questions.

12. "_____ _____, no see," said Hannah as she came into the office after her long vacation.

13. When the fan met Jenifer Aniston, he _____ _____ hand and didn't let go.

14. John _____ _____ of his partner's plans to embezzle the company's money too late.

16. When he realized it was a sales call, he immediately _____ _____ the phone.

18. The assassination of Kennedy was part of a conspiracy, but no one knows it for _____ _____.

Human Interaction

hit it off (with someone)
to get along well with someone from the onset; build good rapport easily.
llevarse bien con alguien desde el principio; caerse bien.

Ben y Tina hit it off **en la fiesta.**
Ben and Tina hit it off at the party.

get along with
to interact with well; to associate in a friendly manner.
llevarse bien con alguien.

Otto, si no empiezas a get along with **los otros niños, no vas a poder jugar pelota con ellos.**
Otto, if you don't start to get along with the other children, you won't be able to play dodgeball with them.

make friends
to form a relationship with or become friends with someone.
hacerse amigo de alguien.

Jimmy es tan tímido que siempre le ha sido difícil make friends **cuando se traslada a una nueva escuela.**
Jimmy's so shy that it's always hard for him to make friends when he moves to a new school.

get in someone's face
to annoy someone by moving directly in front of them into their personal space and begin to argue or try to start a fight.
enfrentarse a alguien; molestar a alguien al ponerse en frente y discutir o intentar iniciar una pelea.

No get in someone's face **en Nueva York si no quieres terminar peleando.**
Don't get in someone's face in New York unless you are ready to fight.

rub elbows with
to be in close contact with or make friends with.
estar en contacto con alguien o hacerse amigo de alguien; codearse con alguien.
Synonym rub shoulders with.

Como era la hija de un actor famoso, Jan pudo rub elbows with **directores y productores de cine desde que era niña.**

Being the daughter of a famous movie star, Jane was able to rub elbows with movie directors and producers since she was a child.

*These idioms are used for interactions with powerful or important people.
Este modismo se utiliza cuando uno se relaciona con gente de poder o importante.

get together
to gather; to unite or come together.
reunirse con alguien.

Oye Ben, vamos a get together **este fin de semana para tomar una cerveza.**

Hey Ben, let's get together this weekend for a beer.

face to face
in direct view of someone; in person.
cara a cara; en persona.

Si vas a despedir a alguien, es mejor hacerlo face to face.

If you are going to fire someone, it's best to do it face to face.

*This idiom is hyphenated when used before a noun as an adjective.
Este modismo se utiliza con guiones cuando se emplea como adjetivo, delante de un sustantivo.

tie the knot
to get married.
casarse; contraer matrimonio.

Terry y Jane decidieron tie the knot **y volaron a Las Vegas para una ceremonia matrimonial rápida.**

Terry and Jane decided to tie the knot and flew off to Las Vegas for a quick wedding ceremony.

*In this idiom, the knot signifies the bond of marriage.
En este modismo, el nudo significa el lazo del matrimonio.

on the rocks
in serious trouble; in danger of failing.
con problemas; en peligro de fallar.

Debido a que Jerry siempre está viajando por negocios, su matrimonio con Amy está on the rocks.

With Jerry always away on business, his marriage to Amy is on the rocks.

break it off
to discontinue a relationship; to break the bond of a relationship.
romper una relación.
Synonym split up; break up.

Terrance quiere break it off **con su novia, pero no sabe cómo decírselo.**

Terrance wants to break it off with his girlfriend, but he doesn't know how to tell her.

split up
to separate; to end a relationship.
separarse; terminar una relación.

¿Por qué quieres split up **de tu esposo, Gale? Él te trata con tanta dulzura.**
Why would you want to split up with your husband, Gale? He's so sweet to you.

**start off on
the wrong foot**
to begin a relationship or situation
on a bad note.
comenzar mal; comenzar con el pie
izquierdo.
*Antonym start off on the right foot.

Vanessa start off on the wrong foot **con su nuevo jefe al llegar tarde el primer día.**
Vanessa started off on the wrong foot with her new boss when she was late the first day.

Fill in the blanks with the appropriate idioms.

01 The Dawsons _____ up temporarily, with the possibility of getting back together.

Los Dawson se separaron por un tiempo, pero con de posibilidad de volver en un futuro.

02 Her brother was so outgoing, he could _____ _____ with anyone he met.

Su hermano era tan extrovertido que podía llevarse bien con cualquiera que conocía.

03 Henry got _____ _____ with a pretty girl last weekend and we haven't seen him since.

Henry se reunió con una linda muchacha el fin de semana pasado y no lo hemos visto desde entonces.

04 Adam never _____ it _____ with his wife's parents, but he always tried to be pleasant to them anyway.

Adam nunca llegó a llevarse muy bien con sus suegros pero siempre intentó ser agradable de todos modos.

05 It has been very hard on Kirk since she _____ _____ off. He's still in love with his ex-girlfriend and can't bear to be apart from her.

Ha sido muy duro para Kirk desde que rompió con ella. Sigue enamorado de su ex–novia y no soporta estar sin ella.

06 Geronimo, the famous Indian, liked to fight _____ to _____ to see the fear in his enemy's eyes.

A Gerónimo, el famoso indio, le gustaba pelear cara a cara para poder ver el miedo en los ojos de sus enemigos.

07 If you _____ off on _____ _____ _____, it's not easy to change someone's first impression.

Si empiezas mal, no es muy fácil cambiar esa primera impresión que dejas en la persona.

08 Sarah and her sister just never seem to _____ _____ with each other. They fight like cats and dogs.

Parece que Sarah y su hermana nunca se llevan bien: pelean como perros y gatos.

09 If you want to _____ _____ _____ interesting and influential people, you should go to the governor's ball.

Si quieres codearte con gente interesante y poderosa, debes ir al baile del gobernador.

10 I was in an accident yesterday, and the taxi driver who caused the accident kept trying to _____ in my _____ and start a fight.

Tuve un accidente ayer y el taxista causante del accidente intentó varias veces alzar la voz y comenzar a pelear.

11 Fred and Wilma _____ the _____ ten years ago and have been happily married ever since.

Fred y Wilma contrajeron matrimonio hace diez años y han estado felizmente casados desde entonces.

12 Tino's relationship with his girlfriend has been _____ _____ _____ ever since they started arguing about money.

La relación de Tino con su novia ha estado andando mal desde que empezaron a discutir por dinero.

Answers 1. split (up) 2. make friends 3. (got) together 4. hit (it) off 5. broke it (off) 6. face (to) face 7. start (off on) the wrong foot 8. get along (with) 9. rub elbows with 10. get (in my) face 11. tied (the) knot 12. on the rocks

Read the following story and refer to the questions below.

- The Right Foot

When I was younger, life was all about making friends, trying to get along with my siblings* and having fun. These days it seems to be all about trying to hit it off in business by rubbing elbows with the "right" people. I still manage to get together with friends once in a while, but I'm mostly busy trying to get ahead. They say, "If you start off on the wrong foot in the business world, it's hard to recover."

Then there's the problem of relationships... I was hoping to tie the knot with my girlfriend this year, but now we've split up. She kept getting in my face about my work schedule. I tried to tell her that I have to do business face to face as a salesman, but she never understands. I guess that's why we broke it off. Even my coworkers' relationships are all on the rocks. Maybe I really need to change my job!

*siblings hermanos

Questions about the story

1. What does the writer miss?

2. What does he do these days?

3. What kind of business is he in?

4. How is his relationship?

5. What did he plan to do? How did that change?

6. Why did he separate from his girlfriend?

7. How are his coworkers' relationships?

8. What does he think he should do in the end?

Questions for discussion

1. How do you make friends? Is it easy for you to hit it off?

2. Have you ever started off on the wrong foot with someone? How? And what did you do about it?

3. If you really hit it off with someone, how long would you need to date before you would tie the knot?

4. In your country, what can you do if your marriage is on the rocks?

5. What kind of people would you like to rub elbows with? Where would you go to meet them?

Con el pie derecho

Cuando era joven, mi vida era hacer amigos, tratar de llevarme bien con mis hermanos y divertirme. Ahora parece que lo más importante es tener éxito en los negocios y codearse con personas "importantes". De vez en cuando me encuentro con mis amigos, pero normalmente estoy trabajando para abrirme camino. Dicen que, "Si comienzas mal en el mundo de los negocios, es muy difícil recuperarse."

También está el problema de las relaciones… esperaba casarme con mi novia este año, pero rompimos. Ella siempre discutía conmigo sobre mis horarios de trabajo. Intenté explicarle que tengo que hacer negocios cara a cara como vendedor, pero nunca entendió. Probablemente esa sea la razón por la que rompimos. Hasta las relaciones de mis colegas andan mal. Tal vez necesito cambiar de trabajo.

Family Matters

come from
to be one's birth place or where one has grown up.
lugar donde uno nació o creció.
*__Synonym__ be from.

Los abuelos de Tina come from **Inglaterra. Inmigraron a Canadá después de la Segunda Guerra Mundial.**
Tina's grandparents come from England. They immigrated to Canada after the Second World War.

give birth to
to have a baby; to bear a child.
dar a luz a un bebé.
*__Synonym__ have a boy; have a girl.

La esposa de Tyler give birth to **una nena ayer por la mañana.**
Tyler's wife gave birth to a baby girl early yesterday morning.

flesh and blood
a close or immediate family member; a blood relative.
sangre de mi sangre; familiar directo.

Andy revisó su árbol genealógico, y encontró el flesh and blood **de sus ancestros.**
Andy traced his family tree, and found the flesh and blood of his ancestors.

grow up
to gradually become an adult; to mature.
crecer y llegar a ser adulto; madurar.

Laurence ha madurado y grow up **para ser un buen hombre.**
Laurence has matured, growing up to be a fine young man.

*This idiom is also said to those who act immature. They are told to 'grow up'. Este modismo también se utiliza con personas que no muestran madurez. Se les dice que deben "grow up".

bring up
to feed, raise and educate a child until they are old enough to take care of themselves.
alimentar, criar, y educar a un niño hasta que tenga suficiente edad para cuidarse solo.

powwow
a gathering to discuss certain issues at length and in-depth.
reunión para discutir ciertos temas a fondo.

hand down
to pass an item, usually of some importance, from an older generation to a younger one.
dar en herencia, normalmente algo de importancia que es pasado de una generación a otra.

take after
to be similar to an older member of one's family in appearance, personality or character.
parecerse a alguien de la familia.
Synonym like father, like son: de tal palo tal astilla.

settle down
to start to lead a stable life, usually with a partner.
sentar cabeza; empezar una vida estable con una pareja.

black sheep
a member of the family or group that stands apart in values from the rest.
oveja negra; miembro de la familia o del grupo que es diferente al resto.

hand-me-down
an item of clothing that was worn by an older family member or friend and then given to a younger person to wear.
ropa heredada; ropa usada por alguien mayor heredado a alguien más joven.

Fue fácil bring up a Dean, él era un niño muy obediente.
It was easy to bring up Dean, as he was an obedient child.

Nuestra familia tuvo una powwow por la noche para dialogar sobre las finanzas.
Our family had a powwow last evening to discuss financial matters.

Tom quiere hand down su reloj de bolsillo de oro a su hija cuando cumpla los dieciocho años.
Tom wants to hand down his gold pocket watch to his daughter when she turns eighteen.

George take after su abuelo pues tiene muchas de las mismas características físicas.
George takes after his grandfather, having many of the same physical characteristics.

Cuando encontró a la mujer de sus sueños, Terry decidió settle down y vender su motocicleta.
After finding the girl of his dreams, Terry decided to sell his motorcycle and settle down.

Joe se convirtió en la black sheep de la familia al no casarse y utilizar métodos dudosos para ganarse la vida.
Joe became the black sheep of the family by remaining detached and choosing dubious ways of earning a living.

Jimmy se quejó porque siempre recibió hand-me-down de su hermano mayor.
Jimmy complained because he always received hand-me-downs from his older brother.

Fill in the blanks with the appropriate idioms.

01 Joshua wanted his children to _____ up in the same small town that he did.

Joshua quería que sus hijos crezcan en el mismo pueblo que él.

02 Brenda nominated her brother for the job because she wanted someone who was her own _____ and _____ to be her boss.

Brenda nominó a su hermano para que ocupase el puesto porque quería que alguien de su propia sangre sea su jefe.

03 Damon was hoping to meet a special woman and _____ _____ with her someday.

Damon esperaba conocer a una mujer especial y sentar cabeza con ella.

04 Carrie was excited to have a child, but was dismayed when she found out she was about to _____ _____ to twins.

Carrie estaba emocionada con la idea de que iba a tener un hijo, pero estaba sorprendida al enterarse que iba a dar a luz a gemelos.

05 "What country did you _____ _____?" was the only question that Somi was asked on the first day of school.

"¿De qué país vienes?", fue la única pregunta que le hicieron a Somi el primer día de escuela.

06 It was not easy for her as a single parent to work two jobs and _____ _____ three children by herself.

No era fácil para ella tener dos trabajos y criar tres niños sola.

07 Patrick hoped his son would _____ _____ him and play hockey in college.

Patrick esperaba que su hijo fuese como él y jugara jockey en la universidad.

08 On my dad's side of the family, there is a silver goblet that is traditionally _____ _____ to the oldest son.

Por parte de la familia de mi papá, hay un cáliz plateado que por tradición, se hereda al hijo mayor.

09 Cliff decided that he would only worry about himself, since the whole family thought of him as the _____ _____ anyway.

Cliff decidió que solo se preocuparía por sí mismo, ya que el resto de la familia lo consideraba la oveja negra.

10 Being the youngest of five children, Wesley mostly received _____ - _____ - _____ instead of new clothes.

Al ser el menor de 5 hermanos, Wesley normalmente heredaba ropa usada en vez de ropa nueva.

11 Since the entire family was concerned about Brittany, they got together for a family _____.

Ya que toda la familia se preocupaba por Brittany, se reunieron en consejo de familia.

Answers   1. grow (up)   2. flesh (and) blood   3. settle down   4. give birth (to)   5. come from
6. bring up   7. take after   8. handed down   9. black sheep   10. hand-me-downs   11. powwow

Read the following story and refer to the questions below.

- *Music in their Blood*

Dwayne had come from Chicago, the City of the Blues. He took after his mom and always had a smile on his face, which made him quite likeable. Dwayne dreamed of becoming a professional musician. He grew up in a family of musicians. Both of his grandfathers had been in big bands in the 1940s. Their children had been brought up in houses where everyone learned to play at least one instrument. Dwayne's brother was always the black sheep of the family and refused to try to learn an instrument. Dwayne knew that his father would hand down his grandfather's acoustic guitar to him on his eighteenth birthday. It was one hand-me-down that he did not mind receiving.

Dwayne's parents had met in music school. When they decided to start a family, they agreed that they would bring up their children to share in their love of music. They even had classical music playing while Dwayne's mom gave birth to him. Dwayne hoped someday to settle down with someone who also shared his love for music.

Questions about the story

1. Where did Dwayne come from?

2. Who did he take after?

3. What kind of family did Dwayne grow up in? How was he brought up?

4. Who is considered the black sheep of the family?

5. What is supposed to be handed down to Dwayne on his eighteenth birthday?

6. Why do you think that Dwayne loves music?

7. What kind of person does Dwayne hope to settle down with?

Questions for discussion

1. Where do you come from?

2. Who do you take after more, your mother or your father?

3. Where did you grow up?

4. Where would you like to have grown up?

5. Is there a black sheep in your family? Who? Why?

6. Did you ever receive hand-me-downs?

7. How old should someone be before they settle down?

8. Is it better to bring up a child in the countryside or in the city? Why?

Música en la sangre

Dwayne vino de Chicago, la Ciudad de los Blues. Se parecía a su mama y siempre tenia una sonrisa en los labios por eso era muy agradable. Dwayne soñaba en ser un musico profesional pues creció en una familia de musicos. Sus dos abuelos tocaban en Big Bands en los años 1940. Sus hijos crecieron en una casa en donde todos aprendieron a tocar por lo menos un instrumento. El hermano de Dwayne fue siempre la oveja negra de la familia y rehusaba aprender a tocar un instrumento. Dwayne sabia que su papa le daría por herencia la guitarra acustica del abuelo cuando cumpliera dieciocho años. Era una guitarra usada que no tenia problema en recibir.

Los papas de Dwayne, se conocieron en la escuela de música. Cuando decidieron empezar una familia, se pusieron de acuerdo en criar a sus hijos de manera que amaran la música. Hasta pusieron música clasica en la sala de maternidad donde la mama de Dwayne dio a luz. Dwayne esperaba sentar cabeza algun dia con alguien quien también ame la música.

Dating & Relationships

stand someone up
to not show up for an appointment with little or no prior notice, usually intentionally.
no presentarse a una cita sin previo aviso, generalmente de forma intencional.

Marcy esperó a Eric hasta las 9 p.m. y luego se dio cuenta de que él stand her up.
Marcy waited for Eric until 9 P.M. and then realized he had stood her up. He never came or called.

go out on a date
to go along with someone of the opposite sex in public for a personal meeting.
salir en público con alguien del sexo opuesto para tener un encuentro personal.
Synonym go out with.

Barry quería go out on a date **con la muchacha que había conocido.**
Barry wanted to go out on a date with the girl he had just met.

make out
to kiss and touch someone in a sexual way.
besar y tocar a alguien de manera sexual.

Los padres de Janet habían salido así que ella y Grant make out **en la sala de estar frente a la chimenea.**
Janet's parents were away so she and Grant made out in the family room in front of the fireplace.

break up
to end or to cut off a relationship and stop dating someone.
finalizar o terminar una relación y dejar de salir con alguien.
Noun breakup.
Synonym split up; break it off.

No escribir cartas o llamar fue el principal motivo por el cual Marcy break up **con Matthew.**
Not writing letters or calling was the main reason that Marcy broke up with Matthew.

go steady

to continually date one person; to make a commitment not to date others.

salir continuamente con una persona; comprometerse a no salir con otras personas.

Después de seis meses de salir formalmente, Jim decidió que conocía a Monique lo suficientemente bien como para go steady con ella.

After six months of dating, Jim decided that he knew Monique well enough to go steady with her.

knockout

someone who is extremely attractive.

alguien que es extremadamente atractivo.

Por favor preséntame a tu hermana mayor, es una verdadera knockout y la quiero conocer.

Please introduce me to your older sister. She is a real knockout and I want to meet her!

hot

extremely attractive and sexy.

extremadamente atractivo y sexy.

¡Tom es tan hot que quisiera que fuera mi novio!

Tom is so hot! I wish that he were my boyfriend!

*'Hot' can be used for both men and women.
'Hot' puede ser utilizado para referirse tanto a hombres como mujeres.

get dumped

to have a relationship cut off in a hurtful, uncaring way, disregarding one's feelings.

cuando en una una relación una persona es terminada de manera dolorosa o indiferente sin importar sus sentimientos.

John get dumped por Mary cuando sintió que la había tratado injustamente.

John got dumped by Mary when she felt he had treated her unfairly.

ex-boyfriend

a former boyfriend.

ex novio.

*Synonym old flame.

Barbara nunca olvidó la manera en que su ex-boyfriend la maltrató.

Barbara never forgot how her ex-boyfriend mistreated her.

*Other words such as, girlfriend, husband, wife, or fiance may also be attached to this prefix. (ex- girlfriend, husband, wife, fiance.)
Este prefijo se puede unir a otras palabras como novia, marido, esposa, o prometida (ex-novia, ex-marido, ex-esposa, ex-prometida).

set up

to prearrange a meeting of two people; to introduce two people with the expectation that they will end up dating.

arreglar una reunión entre dos personas; presentar a dos personas con el fin de que tengan una cita.

*Synonym fix up.

Frank le pidió a su hermana que le set up a la hermana de su novio.

Frank asked his sister to set him up with her boyfriend's sister.

old flame

a previous boyfriend or girlfriend.
novio o novia anterior.
Synonym ex-boyfriend; ex-girlfriend.

make up

to reconcile after a verbal quarrel or argument.
reconciliarse tras una pelea o discusión verbal.

blind date

a first-time date by way of introduction through a third person; a date with someone that one has not met or even seen.
primera cita a través de una presentación de una tercera persona; una cita con alguien que no se conoce o se ha visto.

Sue se sintió incómoda viendo a su old flame Dan en la fiesta por eso se fue temprano a casa.

Sue felt uncomfortable seeing her old flame, Dan, at the party, so she went home early.

Tras un desacuerdo, Carol y Dean make up y están saliendo nuevamente juntos.

After a disagreement, Carol and Dean made up with each other and are now going out again.

Alex nunca había conocido a Judy hasta que tuvieron una blind date.

Alex never met Judy until they went out on a blind date.

F ill in the blanks with the appropriate idioms.

01 Mitchell tried to build up enough courage to ask Jessica to _____ _____ on a date with him.

Mitchell intentó armarse de suficiente valor para invitar a Jessica a tener una cita con él.

02 Even as teenagers, Billy and Sue were not shy to _____ _____ on the dance floor.

Incluso como adolescentes, Billy and Sue no tenían vergüenza de besarse en la pista de baile.

03 Leslie was famous for setting her friends up on _____ _____.

Leslie era famosa por planificar citas a ciegas para sus amigas.

04 Renee knew she was a _____, so she walked into the night club with confidence.

Renee sabía que era una chica hermosa por lo tanto entró al club nocturno con confianza.

05 Andrew wanted his friend Kevin to _____ him _____ with Kevin's cousin from out of town.

Andrew quería que su amigo Kevin lo presentara a su prima que no era de la ciudad.

06 After waiting at the table by himself for an hour, Brent accepted the fact that his blind date had _____ _____ _____.

Tras esperar en la mesa durante una hora, Brent aceptó el hecho de que su cita a ciegas lo había dejado plantado.

07 Rachel ran into an _____ _____ from college while she was at the concert with her husband.

Rachel se encontró con un antiguo amor de la universidad mientras estaba en el concierto con su esposo.

08 Joany had an awful feeling that her boyfriend was going to _____ _____ with her on the weekend.

Joany tenía el terrible presentimiento que su novio iba a terminar con ella el fin de semana.

09 Someday, I want to have a boyfriend like Keith. He is so _____.

Algun dia quiero tener un novio como tenía Kieth, está tan guapo.

10 Dan and Martha felt so serious about each other, that they decided to go _____.

Dan y Martha sentían algo tan serio entre ellos, que decidieron tener una relación estable.

11 Joy wasn't very excited about going to the school dance because she knew that her _____-boyfriend would be there.

Joy no estaba muy entusiasmada de ir al baile de la escuela porque sabía que su ex-novio estaría ahí.

12 After being angry at each other for hours, the young couple finally decided to _____ up.

Después de estar enojados durante horas, la joven pareja finalmente decidió reconciliarse.

13 After cutting off several relationships with girlfriends, Ryan was devastated to get _____ by the only girl that he really cared for.

Después de terminar varias relaciones, Ryan estaba desvastado de ser terminado por la única muchacha que realmente le interesaba.

Answers 1. go out (on a date) 2. make out 3. blind dates 4. knockout 5. set (him) up 6. stood (him) up 7. old flame 8 break up 9. hot 10. (go) steady 11. ex-(boyfriend) 12. make (up) 13. (get) dumped

Read the following story and refer to the questions below.

- *(Not) Married with (no) children*

Joy was only thirty-five, but she felt old. She always thought that by the time she was thirty, she would be married with children. She could not understand it. She was a knockout, yet she didn't have many men asking her out. She had to rely on her married friends and even her mother to set her up. Joy did not enjoy going on blind dates. She would rather call up her old flame Rico for an evening out, than go out with someone she didn't know. As Joy recalls, he was really hot!

If someone set her up on a blind date, she would usually meet the person at least once. Sometimes, to get out of a blind date she wasn't enjoying, Joy would agree to meet the man for a second date and then leave. When the day of the second date would come, she would sometimes stand the man up. It was easier than leading the person on and having to break up with him later.

Often when she was feeling lonely, she would dream of her boyfriend from college. She loved thinking of the time when they were going steady. She always wished she had tried harder to make up with him. Now, he was happily married and she was stuck in a vicious dating circle*.

---

*vicious circle círculo vicioso

Questions about the story

1. How old is Joy?

2. How does she find someone to date?

3. Does she like going on blind dates?

4. What does she remember about her old flame?

5. How did Joy sometimes get out of dating someone?

6. What did she like thinking about?

7. What does she seem to regret?

Questions for discussion

1. Have you ever been dumped?

2. Have you ever dumped someone? How did you do it?

3. Do you ever think about your ex-boyfriend or ex-girlfriend?

4. Have you ever seen an old flame with another partner in public?

5. What do you think about blind dates?

6. What is your idea of a perfect date?

7. Did your parents ever catch you making out with a boyfriend or girlfriend?

8. Have you ever been stood up or stood someone else up? Why?

(No) Casado con (sin) hijos

Joy tenía solamente treinta y cinco años pero se sentía vieja. Siempre pensó que cuando tuviera treinta, estaría casada con hijos. No podía comprenderlo. Era un bombón, aún así no había muchos hombres que la invitaran a salir. Tenía que depender de sus amigas casadas e incluso de su madre para que le arreglen citas. A Joy no le gustaba tener citas a ciegas. Prefería llamar a Rico, su amor de antaño para una salida por la noche y luego salir con alguien que no conociera. Según recordaba Joy, ¡realmente era muy guapo!

Si alguien le arreglaba una cita a ciegas, generalmente se encontraba con esa persona al menos una vez. A veces, para salir de una cita a ciegas que no estaba disfrutando, Joy se ponía de acuerdo con la persona para tener una segunda cita y luego se iba. Cuando llegaba el momento de esa segunda cita, algunas veces no se presentaba. Era más sencillo que engañar a esa persona y luego tener que terminar la relación.

A menudo cuando se sentía sola, soñaba con su novio de la universidad. Amaba pensar en los momentos en que estaban tomando las cosas con seriedad. Siempre deseó haber intentado con más ahínco regresar con el. Ahora, él estaba felizmente casado y ella se encontraba enganchada en un círculo vicioso de citas."

Visiting Friends

come over
for a guest to visit at one's house.
cuando un invitado visita la casa de uno.

Horas después del nacimiento de su primer hijo, Andrea estaba entusiasmada porque su madre come over y ver el bebé.
Only hours after the birth of her first child, Andrea was excited for her mother to come over and see the baby.

drop in on
to visit someone without prior notice.
visitar a alguien sin previo aviso.
****Synonym*** drop by.

El director de la escuela decidió drop in on la nueva maestra para ver si necesitaba alguna ayuda.
The school principal decided to drop in on the new teacher to see if she needed any assistance.

show someone in
to politely lead a guest into one's home or work.
guiar amablemente a una visita por la casa o trabajo.

Matt y Sunny show Jay and Christa in en la fiesta y les presentaron a unos amigos nuevos.
Matt and Sunny showed Jay and Christa in at the party and introduced them to some new friends.

stopover
a break in one's journey.
hacer escala en un viaje.
****Verb*** stop over to visit for a period of time.
visitar por un periodo de tiempo.

Frank viajó en avión desde Chicago a Dallas con un stopover de dos horas en Atlanta.
Frank traveled by plane from Chicago to Dallas with a two-hour stopover in Atlanta.

swing by
to visit for a short time.
visitar por un periodo corto de tiempo.

Después del trabajo, Paul swing by **por la escuela para recoger a su hijo quien había culminado su práctica de futbol.**
After work, Paul swung by the school to pick up his son who had just finished football practice.
* To 'swing by' is generally for the purpose of picking something or someone up. 'Swing by' generalmente se refiere cuando uno busca a alguien o algo.

get together
to have an informal social gathering or meeting.
tener una reunión social informal.
* **Noun** get-together.

Todos nuestros amigos get together **para una barbacoa.**
All of our friends got together for a BBQ.

pay a visit
to formally call on or stop at someone's house or place of business.
llamar formalmente o ir a la casa o lugar de trabajo de alguien.

Tom y Sarah pay a visit **la familia de Sarah cuando anunciaron sus planes de casarse.**
Tom and Sarah paid a visit to Sarah's family when they announced their plans to get married.

make someone feel at home
to make someone feel comfortable and relaxed.
hacer sentir a alguien a gusto y relajado.

Andy realmente make us feel at home **en su fiesta. Es un gran anfitrión.**
Andy really made us feel at home at his party. He is a great host.

have a seat
to sit down on a chair or some piece of furniture.
sentarse en una silla o sobre algún mueble.
* **Synonym** grab a seat; take a chair. (informal)

¡Entra! have a seat **en la sala de estar y siéntete como en tu casa.**
Come in! Have a seat in the living room and make yourself feel at home.

visit with
to meet and spend time talking with someone.
encontrarse y pasar el tiempo charlando con alguien.

Yo visit with **la tía Doreen el verano pasado. Charlamos y pasamos un rato agradable juntas.**
I visited with Aunt Doreen last summer. We talked and had a great time together.

make oneself feel at home
to make oneself feel comfortable and relaxed, as if at one's home.
sentirse cómodo y relajado, como en la propia casa.
Synonym make oneself at home.

be my guest
to give permission to someone to do something freely.
dar permiso a alguien para hacer algo libremente.

see someone out
to politely lead a guest out of ones' home or work.
guiar gentilmente a un invitado fuera de la casa o trabajo de uno; acompañar hasta la salida.

Nick make himself feel at home al sacarse los zapatos, disfrutar de una cerveza y ver TV antes de ir a dormir.
Nick made himself feel at home by kicking off his shoes, enjoying a beer and watching TV before going to bed.

"¿Te importaría si uso el teléfono?" "Por supuesto que no. be my guest."
"Do you mind if I use the phone?"
"Of course not. Be my guest."

Al finalizar la reunión, Chris see the new client out.
At the end of the meeting, Chris saw the new client out.

bye~

Fill in the blanks with the appropriate idioms.

01 Frank thought that he should _____ a _____ to his friend Roman on his birthday.

Frank pensó que debía pasar a visitar a su amigo Román por su cumpleaños.

02 Steve's wife told him that he should stay and _____ _____ her parents instead of watching football on TV.

La esposa de Steve le dijo que debería quedarse y charlar con sus padres en vez de mirar fútbol en la televisión.

03 Paul asked Jen if she would like to come _____ to his place for dinner.

Paul le preguntó a Jen si le gustaría ir a su casa para cenar.

04 Doreen made a note for herself so she would remember to _____ _____ the pharmacy on the way home.

Doreen se escribió una nota para recordar pasar por la farmacia camino a casa.

05 Gayle quickly _____ _____ _____ at _____ by rearranging the hotel room furniture to an arrangement that she felt more comfortable with.

Gayle rápidamente se sintió como en casa al arreglar los muebles de la habitación del hotel de manera que se sintiera más cómoda.

06 Antoine did not like people to _____ in _____ him without calling first.

A Antoine no le gustaba que la gente se presentara sin llamarlo antes.

07 Amanda was hoping that her parents would _____ _____ at her apartment with a care package of food and money on their way to Florida.

Amanda esperaba que sus padres visitaran su apartamento trayendo un paquete de comida y dinero en su camino a Florida.

08 Everyone was planning to get _____ on Saturday evening at the casino.

Todos estaban planeando reunirse en el casino el sábado por la noche.

09 Breanne asked her guests to _____ a _____ in the living room as they entered.

Breanne pidió a sus invitados que tomaran asiento en la sala de estar a medida que entraran.

10 The smell of roast beef in the oven made Peter remember his childhood. It also made him _____ at _____.

El aroma del estofado en el horno hizo a Peter recordar su infancia y también lo hizo sentir como en casa.

11 Alan's job at the party was to _____ the guests _____ as they arrived.

El trabajo de Alan en la fiesta fue hacer sentir a los invitados como en casa mientras iban llegando.

12 Tom made sure that he _____ his guests _____ when they left his party.

Tom se aseguró de acompañar a sus invitados a la puerta cuando se despedian de la fiesta.

13 When I asked Sam if I could open his bottle of whisky, he said, "_____ my _____."

Cuando le pregunté a Sam si podía abrir su botella de whisky, él dijo, "por supuesto".

Answers **1.** pay (a) visit **2.** visit with **3.** (come) over **4.** swing by **5.** made herself feel (at) home **6.** drop (in) on **7.** stop over **8.** (get) together **9.** have (a) seat **10.** (made him) feel (at) home **11.** show (the guests) in **12.** saw (his guests) out **13.** Be (my) guest.

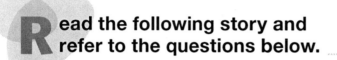 ead the following story and refer to the questions below.

- Old Friends

The Christmas holidays were Frank's favorite time of year. He enjoyed having the extra time to pay a visit to friends he didn't get to see while he was working. On the Friday before the holiday weekend, Frank planned to swing by the town he grew up in and drop in on his childhood best friend, Enzio, and his family.

Frank would usually get together with Enzio on the day after Christmas, but this year Frank had some friends from out of town coming over, so he chose to make this year's visit short.

After arriving, it did not take Frank long to make himself at home at Enzio's house. Minutes after Enzio's wife, Laura, showed him into the living room, the kids were using him as a swing set. Laura asked Frank to have a seat on the couch, but the children pulled him up right away. Enzio's family really made Frank feel at home. He came from a family where all of the children had grown up and moved away. After visiting for a few hours, Frank decided to say goodbye and see himself out.

Questions about the story

1. Why did Frank enjoy the Christmas holidays so much?
2. What did he plan to do on the Friday before the holidays?
3. When did he usually get together with Enzio?
4. Does Frank feel comfortable at Enzio's house? Explain.
5. What were the kids doing with Frank?
6. Did Enzio see Frank out?

Questions for discussion

1. When do you have people over at your home to visit?
2. Do you ever drop in on a friend unexpectedly?
Why or why not?
3. What can you do to make yourself feel at home in someone else's house?
4. What can you say or do to make a guest feel at home in your house?
5. Should you always see your guest out?
6. Among your friends, who do you enjoy visiting the most? Why?
7. Who are some people that you should visit with even though you might not enjoy the visit?

Viejos amigos

Para Frank, las fiestas navideñas eran su época favorita del año. Disfrutaba tener tiempo libre para visitar a sus amigos que no podía ver mientras trabajaba. El viernes anterior al fin de semana de fiestas, Frank planeó pasar por el pueblo en donde creció y sorprender con una visita a su mejor amigo de la infancia Enzio y su familia.

Generalmente Frank solía reunirse con Enzio el día después de Navidad, pero este año Frank tenía la visita de algunos amigos que no eran de la ciudad, así que decidió acortar la visita este año.

Después de llegar, a Frank no le llevo mucho tiempo sentirse como en casa. Minutos después de que la esposa de Enzio lo guió a la sala, los niños lo estaban utilizando a él como columpio. Laura le pidió a Frank que tomase asiento en el sofá pero los chicos lo sacaron de inmediato. La familia de Enzio realmente lograba que Frank se sintiese en casa. Él provenía de una familia donde todos los hijos ya habían crecido y se habían ido. Después de haberlos visitado por un par de horas, Frank decidió despedirse y dirigirse a la salida.

have someone over
to invite someone to one's home.
invitar a alguien a la casa de uno.

Tom quería conocer mejor a Doreen de manera que have her over **a cenar.**
Tom wanted to get to know Doreen better, so he decided to have her over for dinner.

how about
used for suggesting, proposing or offering something to someone informally.
se utiliza para sugerir, proponer u ofrecer algo a alguien de manera informal.

"¿how about **venir con nosotros para pasar las vacaciones?", Mary preguntó a su amiga.**
"How about coming along with us on vacation?" Mary asked her friend.

take a rain check
to delay an invitation until the next available time.
postergar una invitación hasta tener disponibilidad de tiempo.

Ryan invitó a Mary a tomar café, pero como aún ella no había terminado su trabajo le preguntó si podía take a rain check.
Ryan asked Mary out for coffee, but she was not done with her work so she asked him if she could take a rain check.

be free
to have nothing important to do; to have no plans.
no tener nada importante que hacer; no tener planes.

Los sábados Greg no trabaja por lo tanto be free **para hacer lo que le plazca.**

On Saturday, Greg does not work, so he is free to do as he pleases.

turn down
to reject an offer or proposal.
rechazar una oferta o propuesta.

Tina turn down la idea de Jay referente a ir al cine juntos el viernes por la noche.

Tina turned down Jay's idea to go to the movies together on Friday night.

tag along
to follow another person or group, without invitation or acceptance from the person or group.
acompañar a otra persona o grupo sin invitación o aceptación de la persona o grupo.

El hermano mayor de John no fue invitado a patinar sobre hielo , pero tag along de todas maneras.

John was not invited to go ice skating with his big brother, but he tagged along anyway.

ask someone out
to invite someone to come with you to a place.
invitar a alguien a ir con uno a algún lugar.

Sandy quería ask Tony out pero no lo hizo porque era muy tímida.

Sandy wanted to ask Tony out, but she didn't because she was too shy.

take someone up on something
to accept an invitation, proposal or an informal offer.
aceptar una invitación, propuesta u oferta informal.

Al principio Sally no quería ir, pero luego decidió take Tom up on la propuesta de Tom de cenar juntos en un restaurante romántico.

At first Sally did not want to go, but then she decided to take Tom up on his offer to have dinner together at a romantic restaurant.

go along (with)
to support an idea by joining and following a leader or suggestion.
apoyar una moción o idea uniéndose al líder o a la sugerencia.

Jessica go along with Erica y Jen al centro comercial para hacer compras.

Jessica went along with Erica and Jen to the mall to go shopping.

shoot someone down
to reject someone in an unkind way.
rechazar a alguien de manera poco amable.

Después de que Jim hiciera un comentario ofensivo sobre el vestido de Amy, ella shoot him down con su sagacidad y se fue a casa.

After Jim made an offensive comment about Amy's dress, she shot him down with her quick wit and went home.

F ill in the blanks with the appropriate idioms.

01 "_____ _____ going for a walk in the woods?" asked Samuel.
"¿Qué te parece si vamos a caminar por el bosque? preguntó Samuel.

02 Michelle told Peter she would have to take a _____ _____ for their date on Friday, as something else had come up.
Michelle le dijo a Peter que tendría que cambiar la cita del viernes ya que surgió un imprevisto.

03 Ethan asked Christina if she was _____ on Saturday to go to a movie.
Ethan le preguntó a Christina si estaba libre el sábado para ir al cine.

04 Janet usually _____ down about one date request per week.
Generalmente Janet rechaza una cita por semana.

05 Rob needed to build up some courage to _____ Heather _____ on a date, so he had a few drinks before approaching her.
Rob necesitaba armarse de valor para invitar a Heather a salir, así que tomó algunos tragos antes de aproximarse a ella.

06 Since he was almost all out of money, Jack decided to _____ Liz up _____ her offer to pay for their dinner.
Ya que casi no tenía dinero, Jack decidió aceptar la oferta de Liz de pagar la cena.

07 Jeff was hoping to _____ a few friends _____ to watch the World Cup soccer match at his house.
Jeff esperaba invitar a algunos amigos a ver el partido de fútbol de la Copa Mundial en su casa.

08 Alyssa always tried to _____ _____ with her older sisters, even though at times she was not welcome.
Alyssa siempre trataba de acompañar a sus hermanas mayores aunque a veces no era bien recibida.

09 Harold needed something smooth to say to the women at the club so he wouldn't get _____ _____ .
Harold necesitaba decirles algo refinado a las mujeres en el club para que no lo rechacen sin miramientos.

10 Simon didn't know who the party was for or why his friends were going, but he decided to just go _____ with his friends anyway.
Simón no sabía para quién era la fiesta o por qué razón sus amigos estaban yendo pero decidió seguirles la corriente de todas maneras.

Answers 1. How about 2. (take a) rain check 3. (was) free 4. turns (down) 5. ask (Heather) out 6. take (Liz up) on 7. have (a few friends) over 8. tag along 9. shot down 10. (go) along (with)

Read the following story and refer to the questions below.

- Second Chance

Winston was excited about the upcoming holiday weekend. He asked his parents if he could have friends over to their cottage* while they were out of town. Winston's parents had agreed the week before, so he asked Mai Ling if she would be free to come over.

It took some courage to ask Mai Ling out again. She had turned him down two other times this year. Winston hated that the whole school knew that Mai Ling had shot him down the last time he asked her out. She really only agreed to go to the cottage this time because he had invited a group of people.

Mai Ling took her friend Sarah up on her offer to drive both ways. Sarah's older sister took a rain check on the weekend festivities* because she had to work, but Sarah's younger sister Sierra begged to tag along with her for the weekend. Now is his chance to show her what a nice guy he is.

---

*cottage casa de campo *festivities festividades.

Questions about the story

1. Why was Winston excited about the upcoming weekend?
2. Who did Winston ask if she was free to come over?
3. Was it easy for Winston to ask Mai Ling out? Why?
4. How did Mai Ling reject Winston the last time he asked her out?
5. Why did Mai Ling agree this time?
6. What did Mia Ling's friend Sarah offer to do?
7. Will Sarah's older sister be going to the cottage for the weekend?
8. Who will go instead of Sarah's older sister?

Questions for discussion

1. How do you ask out people in your country?
What do you say?

2. Have you ever been rejected or shot down? Explain.

3. Are you often free to go out with friends?

4. How often do you have friends over to your house?

5. Do you ever tag along with other friends? If so, when?

6. How do you feel just before you ask someone out?

7. Is it common for women to ask men out in your country?
What do you think about this?

Una segunda oportunidad

Winston estaba entusiasmado por el fin de semana feriado que se aproximaba. Le preguntó a sus padres si podía invitar a unos amigos a la casa de campo* mientras ellos no estaban en casa. Los padres de Winston accedieron la semana anterior así que llamó a Mai Ling para ver si estaba libre para venir.

Tuvo que armarse de mucho valor para pedirle a Mai Ling que saliera nuevamente con él pues ya lo había rechazado dos veces este año. Winston odiaba que toda la escuela supiera que Mai Ling lo había rechazado sin miramientos la última vez que la invitó a salir. La realidad es que esta vez accedió a ir a la casa de campo porque él había invitado a un grupo de personas.

Mai Ling aceptó la propuesta de su amiga Sarah de conducir de ida y vuelta. La hermana mayor de Sarah faltó a las festividades del fin de semana* porque tenía que trabajar, pero Sierra, su hermana menor, le rogó que la llevara el fin de semana. Esta es la oportunidad de demostrarle a Mai Ling qué tipo es.

Chapters ⑯ - ⑳

Review Chapters 16-20 and fill in the crossword below.

Answers → P.173

Across

01. When Sam asked if he could get a beer from the fridge, I said _____ _____ _____.

05. I _____ _____ with Rob in kindergarten and have been close to him ever since.

08. When he became famous, he started to rub _____ with important people.

09. You should confront them _____ _____ _____.

11. Jack and Jill _____ _____ _____ on the hill together.

13. Jon is at the door. Go _____ him _____.

14. Bill went to the hospital to _____ _____ _____ to his sick friend Ted.

17. Cliff was the _____ _____ of the family as he didn't study medicine.

18. The smell of fresh baked cookies always makes me _____ _____ _____.

19. family & blood relatives

21. The kids were _____ _____ by a loving family.

22. After waiting for an hour, Bobby realized his date had _____ _____ _____.

23. Can I _____ _____ with you to Jon's?

24. Sarah took a _____ _____ on the party because she was too tired to go.

25. Tina _____ _____ Jay's invitation to dinner because he was weird.

Down

02. Stan and Mary liked each other so much, that they decided to _____ _____.

03. After the argument, the young couple decided to _____ up again.

04. Jon & Meg think it's rude to _____ _____ on them without calling first, but I love it when you stop by.

06. Bill called an _____ _____ from college when he was back in town to see if she was still single.

07. to be similar to an older member of one's family in appearance, personality or character

10. Fred and Wilma _____ _____ _____ ten years ago and have been happily married ever since.

12. Tom asked his parents if he could _____ friends _____ while they were out of town.

15. After finding the girl of his dreams, Terry decided to sell his motorcycle and _____ _____.

16. Harold needed something to say so women at the club wouldn't _____ him _____.

20. Be nice to Ryan. He got _____ by the his girlfriend last weekend.

Relaxing 21

take it easy
to rest or relax; to refrain from working too hard or getting too angry.
descansar o relajarse; abstenerse de trabajar demasiado fuerte o de enojarse.

Estoy preocupado por Richard. Ha estado trabajando muy duro. Necesita take it easy **de vez en cuando.**
I'm worried about Richard. He has been working too hard. He needs to take it easy once in a while.
* This idiom is often used to calm someone who is angry or overly excited.
Este modismo es a menudo utilizado para calmar a alguien que está enojado o muy ansioso.

take a nap
to sleep for a short period of time.
dormir durante un período corto de tiempo; dormir una siesta.
*Synonym get forty winks; take a snooze; have a siesta; catnap.

Cuando Charles venga a casa estará cansado y deseará take a nap **antes de cenar.**
When Charles comes home he will be tired and will want to take a nap before dinner.

daydream
to unknowingly have a series of pleasant thoughts pass through one's mind while awake that are unrelated to what is happening at the time.
tener, sin darse cuenta, una serie de pensamientos placenteros mientras uno está despierto, los cuales no están relacionados con lo que está pasando en ese momento.

A Lola le gustan mucho los muchachos. Pasa demasiado tiempo daydream **con ellos durante clase.**
Lola likes boys too much. She spends too much time daydreaming about them during class.
* Daydreaming is done only in the daytime.
Daydreaming solo sucede durante el día.

kick back

to take a step away from a busy life and relax.

apartarse de una vida ocupada y relajarse.

Synonym chill: to relax (slang).

Cuando kick back en el trabajo, pongo los pies sobre el escritorio y me recuesto en la silla.

When I kick back at work, I put my feet on the desk and lean back in my chair.

*This idiom is often used with 'and relax'. One usually does both at the same time. Este modismo es a menudo utilizado con "and relax". La persona generalmente hace las dos cosas al mismo tiempo.

take a break

to stop an activity to rest.

hacer una pausa en una actividad para descansar.

Synonym take a breather.

Hemos estado trabajando toda la mañana. take a break por un rato y luego volvamos a trabajar.

We've been working all morning. Let's take a break for a little while and then get back to work.

lounge around

to spend time in a relaxed way, sitting or lying somewhere and doing very little.

pasar el tiempo de manera relajada, sentado o acostado en algún lugar y haciendo pocas cosas.

Los domingos, me gusta lounge around por la casa en bata.

On Sundays, I like to lounge around the house in my bathrobe.

take a load off

to sit down and relax; to give up some heavy burden.

sentarse y relajarse; dejar alguna carga pesada.

Después de trabajar todo el día, la única cosa que Steve deseaba hacer era sentarse y take a load off.

After working all day, the only thing that Steve wanted to do was to sit down and take a load off.

have free time

to have extra time to rest or do some other activity.

tener tiempo extra para descansar o hacer alguna otra actividad.

Synonym have time on one's hands.

Tengo algo de have free time el jueves por la tarde, ¿deseas que nos encontremos para almorzar?

I have some free time Thursday afternoon; do you want to meet for lunch?

kill time

to use up extra time when one has nothing in particular to do.

utilizar tiempo extra cuando uno no tiene nada en particular para hacer.

Noun time to kill.

Los jueves, tengo media hora entre clases, entonces kill time preparándome para la próxima clase.

On Thursdays, I have a half-hour between classes, so I kill time by preparing for the next class.

loosen up

to release oneself of physical and mental tension; to allow oneself to behave much more freely than usual in order to enjoy oneself.
liberarse de la tensión física y mental; poder comportarse más relajado de lo usual y poder divertirse.
***Synonym** let one's hair down.

Candice necesita loosen up. Es demasiado seria y nunca se divierte.

Candice needs to loosen up. She is too serious and never has any fun.

pass the time

to spend time; to idle away free hours.
pasar el tiempo; estar de ocio durante horas libres; holgazanear.

A Alex le encanta pass the time sentado bajo el gran arce.

Alex loves to pass the time sitting under the big maple tree.

*This idiom can be used when commenting on the enjoyment of spending time as well as discontent for having too much of it.
Este modismo puede ser utilizado para comentar el goce de tener algún tiempo libre, así como el descontento por tener demasiado.

F ill in the blanks with the appropriate idioms.

01 Al and Greg had been working since early in the morning, so they decided to _____ a _____ at 10:00am.

Al y Greg han estado trabajando desde temprano esta mañana, por esta razón decidieron tomarse un descanso a las 10:00 am.

02 The students worked hard in the morning because they were hoping to have some _____ _____ at the end of the school day.

Los estudiantes trabajaron duro en la mañana porque deseaban tener tiempo libre al final de la jornada escolar.

03 Since she was up late the night before, Sue decided to _____ _____ _____ in the afternoon.

Debido a que estuvo despierta hasta tarde la noche anterior, Sue decidió tomar una siesta por la tarde.

04 It was a very hot afternoon, so the soccer coach decided to _____ it _____ on the young players.

Fue una tarde muy calurosa, por lo tanto el entrenador de fútbol decidió no ser muy severo con los jóvenes jugadores.

05 Statistics show that the average attention span for most children is about 3 minutes, after which many children start to _____.

Las estadísticas demuestran que el período promedio de atención para la mayoría de los niños dura alrededor de 3 minutos, después de lo cual muchos niños comienzan a soñar despiertos.

06 Glen had two hours to wait for his flight so he read a book to _____ the _____.

Glen tuvo que esperar dos horas por su vuelo, así que leyó un libro para pasar el tiempo.

07 After a busy day at the office, Ryan had been told by more than one person that he needed to _____ up.

Después de un día ajetreado en la oficina, más de una persona le dijo a Ryan que necesitaba relajarse.

08 With two jobs and three children, it was not very often that Gordon had _____ _____ _____.

Con dos trabajos y tres hijos, a menudo Gordon no tenía tiempo libre.

09 Casey had been working without a day off for over two weeks, so she was planning to _____ _____ and relax while watching the game on Sunday.

Casey ha estado trabajando sin descanso durante dos semanas, por lo que planeaba relajarse mientras miraba el partido el domingo.

10 Instead of shoveling the sidewalk out in the cold, Stanley decided to build a fire, put some comfortable clothes on and _____ _____ the house.

En vez de hacer trabajos con la pala en el frío, Stanley decidió encender la chimenea, ponerse ropa cómoda y holgazanear por la casa.

11 When Sam's friend arrived, he told him to come in, pull up a chair and take

_____ _____ _____.

Cuando el amigo de Sam llegó, le dijo que entrara, que traiga una silla y se quitase un peso de encima.

Answers 1. take (a) break 2. (have some) free time 3. take a nap 4. take (it) easy 5. daydream
6. pass (the) time 7. loosen (up) 8. time to kill 9. kick back 10. lounge around 11. (take) a load off

Read the following story and refer to the questions below.

- *Summer Dreaming*

It was the first day of summer vacation for Floyd. As he sat in the back seat on the long drive to the cottage, he gazed* out the window and began daydreaming. In his daydream, he had a cabin of his own where he could kick back and do whatever he wanted. His sister, who was poking* him in the side, snapped him out of his daydream. Ursula was younger than Floyd by two years.

Floyd hated the fact that he had to pass the time on the way to the cottage playing with his sister in the backseat. He yelled at Ursula to stop, but she yelled right back at him to loosen up and that she was just playing. Floyd's dad pulled the van off the road, so that he could take a break and his mom could drive for a while. His dad knew that his mom was a little nervous about driving on the busy highway so he told her to just take it easy, as they were not in a hurry. Floyd thought about all of the work that was to be done once they reached the cottage and then started daydreaming again.

It often took the whole afternoon to unload the van and open the cottage up, but Floyd was hoping to have some free time before supper to go exploring in the forest. Since his mom knew the way to the cottage, Floyd's dad decided to take a nap for a while. His mom started to think about the cottage. She was hoping to have some time to herself in the evening too. She looked forward to being able to relax and lounge around with a good book. Once they arrived at the cottage, Floyd's dad told his mom to take a load off and sit for a few minutes while he and Floyd unloaded the car. It didn't take long, and then they were all able to kick back and relax.

---

*gazed mirar fijamente *poke dar codazos.

Questions about the story

1. What did Floyd begin to do on the first day of summer vacation?
2. What did he want to do in his own cottage?
3. What did he dislike about traveling to the cottage?
4. Why did Ursula yell at Floyd? What did she say?
5. What did their mother look forward to doing?
6. What did Floyd hope to do before supper?
7. What did his father tell his wife upon arriving?
8. What did they all do in the end?

Questions for discussion

1. When do you usually daydream? Hey! Are you daydreaming now?
2. When do you have a chance to kick back and relax?
3. What do you do to kill time?
    How is killing time different from passing the time?
4. Do you ever lounge around the house? When?
5. How often do you take a break when studying or working on something?
6. What are some ways to loosen up after a long stressful day?

Sueño de verano

Era el primer día de vacaciones de verano para Floyd. Cuando se sentó en el asiento trasero para el largo viaje hacia la casa de campo, miró fijamente* por la ventanilla y comenzó a soñar despierto. En su ensueño tenía una cabaña propia donde podía relajarse y hacer lo que quisiera. Su hermana, quien le daba codazos*, lo despertó de su ensueño. Ursula era dos años menor que Floyd.

Floyd odiaba el hecho de que tenía que pasar el tiempo mientras viajaba a la casa de campo jugando con su hermana en el asiento trasero. Le gritaba a Ursula que pare, pero ella le gritaba que se relaje pues solo estaba jugando. El padre de Floyd sacó la camioneta de la ruta, para poder tomar un descanso y dejar que su madre pudiera manejar un rato. Su padre sabía que su madre estaba un poco nerviosa por tener que conducir en la autopista congestionada así que le dijo que lo tomara con calma, ya que no estaban apurados. Floyd pensaba en todo el trabajo que se debía hacer una vez que llegaran a la casa de campo y entonces comenzó a soñar despierto nuevamente.

Generalmente tomaba toda la tarde descargar la camioneta y abrir la casa de campo, pero Floyd deseaba tener un poco de tiempo libre antes de la cena para ir a explorar el bosque. Ya que su madre sabía el camino a la casa de campo, el padre de Floyd decidió tomar una siesta durante un rato. Su madre comenzó a pensar en la casa de campo. También quería tener un tiempo para ella por la noche: ansiaba poder relajarse, y holgazanear leyendo un buen libro. Una vez que llegaron a la casa de campo, el padre de Floyd le dijo a su madre que se sacara un peso de encima y que se sentara por unos minutos mientras el y Floyd descargaban el auto. No les tomó mucho tiempo y luego pudieron relajarse y descansar.

On Holiday 22

on leave
to be away from work for an extended period of time.
estar de licencia del trabajo durante un periodo extenso de tiempo.

La esposa de Marco ha estado on leave por maternidad durante tres meses. Se espera que vuelva al trabajo la próxima semana.
Marco's wife has been on maternity leave for three months now. She is expected to return to work next week.
This is usually for a specific reason such as maternity, research, or military leave.
Esto es generalmente por una razón específica como maternidad, investigación o servicio militar.

see someone off
to accompany someone to a place of departure to say good-bye and watch them leave.
acompañar a alguien a un lugar de partida para despedirse y verlos partir.

Chuck llevó a su hija y yerno al aeropuerto para see them off a Australia.
Chuck drove his daughter and son-in-law to the airport to see them off to Australia.

have time off
to take time off from work; to have a specific amount of time assigned to not be working.
tener tiempo libre del trabajo; tener una cantidad específica de tiempo asignado para no trabajar.

Jeff le preguntó a su jefe si podía have time off para visitar a su madre en el hospital.
Jeff asked his boss if he could have some time off to visit his mother in the hospital.

take in

to watch or experience some entertainment, sport or particular sight.

ver o experimentar algún entretenimiento, deporte o vista particular.

¿Vas a take in algún musical o espectáculo cuando vayas a Nueva York?

Are you going to take in any musicals or shows when you go to New York?

This idiom is generally used to describe seeing beautiful scenery, but is also used for movies and artistic performances.
Este modismo generalmente se utiliza para describir la vista de un hermoso paisaje pero también se utiliza para cines y espectáculos.

check in

to register as a guest when arriving at a hotel to be given a room key.

registrarse como huésped al llegar a algún hotel para recibir la llave de la habitación.

Synonym check into.

Tan pronto Jacob llegó a Sydney, decidió check in en el hotel para dejar su equipaje.

As soon as Jacob arrived in Sydney, he decided to check in at the hotel to drop off his luggage.

check out (of)

to leave a hotel after paying and returning the room key.

dejar el hotel después de pagar y devolver la llave de la habitación.

Me voy a check out del hotel temprano porque debo tomar el avión.

I'm going to check out of the hotel early because I have a plane to catch.

go away

to leave home in order to spend time somewhere else, usually for a holiday.

dejar la casa para pasar tiempo en otro lugar, generalmente para vacacionar.

Creo que voy a go away por unos días durante el próximo fin de semana largo.

I think that I am going to go away for a few days during the next long weekend.

be booked up

for all available rooms or vacancies to be occupied.

cuando todas las habitaciones disponibles o vacantes están ocupadas.

Ennik sabía que las habitaciones en el popular centro turístico be booked up temprano para el fin de semana feriado.

Ennik knew rooms at the popular resort would be booked up early on the holiday weekend.

wake up call

a telephone call or signal to wake someone in the morning, typically at a hotel.

Chris telefoneó a la recepción del hotel para pedir una wake up call a las 7:00 am.

Chris phoned the front desk at the hotel to ask for a

llamada telefónica o señal para despertar a alguien por la mañana, habitualmente en un hotel.

book something
to arrange to have a seat, room, entertainer, etc. at a particular time in the future.
guardar un asiento, habitación, entretenimiento, etc., en un momento específico en el futuro.

go sightseeing
to visit interesting places, especially when on holiday.
visitar lugares interesantes, especialmente durante las vacaciones; hacer una visita turística.
Synonym take in the sights.
Noun sightseeing.

get back
to return from travel.
regresar de un viaje.

take (time) off
to spend time away from work.
pasar un tiempo fuera del trabajo.

7:00am wake up call.

Una de las maneras más sencillas de book a flight para las vacaciones es utilizando Internet.

One of the easiest ways to book a flight for a vacation is to use the Internet.

It is possible to book seats for travel or entertainment, as well as rooms and venues.

Es posible reservar asientos para viajar o para algún entretenimiento, así también como habitaciones y lugares de encuentro.

Durante las vacaciones nuestra familia solía go sightseeing porque no era muy caro para nuestros padres.

During vacations our family would go sightseeing because it did not cost our parents very much money.

David debía get back a su trabajo en la editorial a las 8:30 de la mañana del lunes.

David had to get back to his job at the publishing company by 8:30 Monday morning.

Philip va a take off un par de días del trabajo después de que su esposa tenga el bebé.

Philip is going to take a couple of days off from work after his wife has their baby.

F ill in the blanks with the appropriate idioms.

01 Ray knew the campsites on the water's edge would be _____ _____ early so he called at the beginning of the season.

Ray sabía que los lugares de camping a orillas del agua estarían reservados con anticipación por lo que decidió llamar a principio de la temporada.

02 When arriving for the convention, the company members had to _____ _____ to get their room keys.

Al llegar a la convención, los miembros de la empresa tuvieron que registrarse para obtener las llaves de la habitación.

03 After the reception, the wedding party went to the airport with the happy couple to _____ them _____ on their honeymoon.

Después de la recepción, la gente que asistió a la fiesta de boda fue al aeropuerto con la feliz pareja para verlos partir a luna de miel.

04 Sally wanted to spend more time with her new baby so she asked to extend her time _____ _____.

Sally deseaba pasar más tiempo con su bebé por lo tanto solicitó que le extendieran la licencia.

05 Burt used the telephone in his hotel room to arrange for an early morning _____ _____ _____.

Burt utilizó el teléfono de su habitación en el hotel para solicitar que lo despierten temprano en la mañana.

06 Each year during the winter break, Tom and Cindy leave their kids with family and _____ _____ to spend some time alone together.

Todos los años durante las vacaciones de invierno, Tom y Cindy dejan a sus hijos con la familia y se van a pasar unos días juntos los dos.

07 At the new Howard Johnson hotel, customers can avoid having to _____ _____ by leaving their key and credit card number in a box in the room.

En el nuevo hotel Howard Johnson, los clientes pueden irse dejando la llave y el número de tarjeta de crédito dentro de una caja en la habitación.

08 When we _____ _____ from grocery shopping on Saturday afternoon, one person usually puts the groceries away while the other makes supper.

Cuando volvemos de comprar de la tienda de comestibles el sábado por la tarde, una persona generalmente guarda las provisiones mientras que la otra prepara la cena.

09 Anna and Lori planned to _____ _____ the Rolling Stones concert in Toronto so they left early to get good seats.

Anna y Lori planearon ir a un concierto de los Rolling Stones en Toronto por lo tanto salieron temprano para obtener buenas ubicaciones.

10 Bob was anxious to learn how much time he would _____ _____ to go on vacation.

Bob estaba ansioso por saber cuánto tiempo tendría libre para irse de vacaciones.

11 Once they arrived in Honolulu, Joy and Amber decided to take a helicopter ride to go _____.

Una vez que llegaron a Honolulú, Joy y Amber decidieron hacer un viaje en helicóptero para visitar lugares de interés.

12 As soon as they decided on their vacation destination, David and Sherri went on the Internet to _____ a flight.

Tan pronto decidieron el destino de sus vacaciones, David and Sherri usaron la Internet para reservar un vuelo.

13 Mark took _____ _____ after his wife had a baby to help out at home.

Mark pidió un descanso después de que su esposa dio a luz para ayudar en casa.

Answers 1. (be) booked up 2. check in 3. see (them) off 4. on leave 5. wake up call 6. go away 7. check out 8. get back 9. take in 10. have off 11. sightseeing 12. book (a flight) 13. (took) time off

Read the following story and refer to the questions below.

- Planning a Trip

Christmas break was getting nearer, so Lou and Melanie decided to sit down in front of the computer and investigate* some vacation destinations. They wanted to go away to someplace warm. After a few hours of research, they decided to book a flight to Mexico. The popular hotels usually book up quickly during the winter months, so Lou and Melanie made reservations right away. Next, they planned some sightseeing activities. Lou wanted to go golfing while Melanie was hoping to take in the dolphin show at the water park. Since they would need to check in at the hotel before participating in any activities, they planned on taking a tour of the area in the afternoon.

Because they had ten days off, they planned to only spend seven days in Mexico and the rest relaxing at home with family. Lou asked his brother Sid if he would be able to take them to the airport to see them off. Sid agreed to drive them, and said that if he were not on leave due to an injury, he and his wife would have enjoyed getting away together with them.

On the last day of their vacation, Melanie and Lou were planning to go snorkeling* in the morning. They knew they would have to get back to the hotel and check out by 11:00 am, so they had to rush a little. In the end, they had a wonderful time, and were ready to get back to family and friends at home.

---

*investigate investigar *snorkel bucear con esnórquel

Questions about the story

1. What did Lou and Melanie want to do for their Christmas vacation?
2. What did they decide to do after a few hours?
3. What usually happens at the popular hotels during the busy winter months?
4. What kind of activities did they plan?
5. What was Melanie hoping to do?
6. What did Sid agree to do for Lou and Melanie?
7. What did the couple have to do after their morning snorkeling activity?

Questions for discussion

1. When do you usually take your vacation?
2. Can you take time off for your vacation whenever you want, or do you have time off only at a certain time of year?
3. Are you the type of person that likes to go sightseeing on vacation?
4. Have you ever gotten a wake up call when you were on vacation?
5. How long does it usually take to check into a hotel?
6. Have you ever booked a flight online?
7. If you could take some time off to go anywhere, where would you go and for how long?

8. What would be your idea of a dream vacation?

Planeando un viaje

Se estaban acercando las fiestas navideñas, así que Lou y Melanie decidieron sentarse frente a la computadora e investigar algunos destinos para las vacaciones. Querían irse de viaje a algún lugar cálido. Después de unas horas de investigación, decidieron comprar un boleto de avión a México. Generalmente los hoteles populares se llenaban rapidamente durante los meses de invierno, por eso Lou y Melanie hicieron reservas de inmediato. Luego, planearon una visita turística. Lou quería ir a jugar al golf mientras que Melanie quería ir a ver un espectáculo de delfines en el parque acuático. Ya que necesitarían registrarse en el hotel antes de participar de cualquier actividad, planearon hacer una visita guiada a la zona por la tarde.

Debido a que tenían diez días libres, planearon pasar solamente siete días en México y el resto de tiempo relajarse en casa con la familia. Lou le pidió a su hermano Sid si podía acompañarlos al aeropuerto para despedirlos. Sid acordó llevarlos y dijo que si él no hubiese tenido licencia por lesiones, él y su esposa habrían disfrutado ese viaje con ellos. En el último día de sus vacaciones, Melanie y Lou estaban planeando bucear con esnorquel por la mañana. Sabían que debían regresar y salir del hotel a las 11:00 am por lo tanto debían apurarse. Al final tuvieron una hermosa estadía pero estaban listos para regresar a casa donde los esperaban su familia y amigos.

Sickness

run a fever
to have a high temperature.
tener temperatura alta.

Los padres de Alex estaban bastante preocupados ya que Alex run a fever **durante tres días sin ningún cambio.**
Alex's parents were quite worried since Alex had been running a fever for three days without any change.

take a turn for the worse
for one's health condition to worsen; for a sickness to decline further.
empeorarse el estado de salud de una persona; agravarse una enfermedad.

Después de la cirugía, la salud de Ed take a turn for the worse **ya que se le desarrolló una infección.**
After the surgery, Ed's health took a turn for the worse when he developed an infection.

feel out of it
not to feel normal or in a sharp mental condition; to feel dazed.
no sentirse normal o en buena condición mental; sentirse aturdido.

Brian feel out of it **después de tomar medicación para el resfrío.**
Brian felt out of it after taking cold medication.

be under the weather
to feel ill or sick.
sentirse enfermo.

Gary no fue a trabajar y se quedó en casa porque be under the weather.
Gary stayed home from work because he was under the weather.

feel/be run down
to feel exhausted physically and mentally; to be in poor condition.
sentirse agotado física y mentalmente; estar en un mal estado.

Trabajar por largas horas y no dormir nunca lo suficiente realmente me hace feel run down.

Working long hours at my job and constantly not getting enough sleep really make me feel run down.

*To be run down is not a condition or state that occurs suddenly. It happens gradually over time and the recovery is also gradual.
'Be run down' no es una condición o estado que ocurre de repente. Sucede gradualmente con el tiempo y la recuperación también es gradual.

sick as a dog
extremely sick.
extremadamente enfermo.

Después de comer en ese restaurante, Matthew se puso sick as a dog.

After eating at that restaurant, Matthew became sick as a dog.

catch a cold
to develop a sickness; to become sick.
desarrollar una enfermedad; enfermarse.
*Synonym come down with (a cold).

Asegúrate de usar un saco al salir o vas a catch a cold.

Make sure you wear a coat when you go outside or you will catch a cold.

feel a cold coming on
to feel as if one is becoming sick or about to become sick.
sentirse como si uno se estuviera enfermando o a punto de enfermarse.

Tom se fue a casa porque dijo que feel a cold coming on y que debía descansar.

Tom went home because he said that he felt a cold coming on and that he should rest.

going around
to be spreading from one person to the next.
que se contagia de una persona a otra

La gripe estaba going around y Bill fue la cuarta persona en su clase en contagiarse.

The flu was going around, and Bill was the fourth person in his class to catch it.

be laid up
to be forced to rest in order to recuperate from a sickness, illness or an injury.
verse forzado a descansar para recuperarse de una enfermedad, o lesión.

Christina be laid up en casa durante cuatro días cuando le dio la gripe. Estaba extremadamente enferma.

Christina was laid up at home for four days when she caught the flu. She was sick as a dog.

run its course
for a sickness to persist for an anticipated period.
cuando una enfermedad persiste por un periodo de tiempo anticipado.

get a checkup
to have a physical examination by a doctor.
hacerse un examen físico con el médico.

get over
to recover and recuperate from illness or sickness.
recuperarse de una enfermedad.

Generalmente lleva alrededor de una semana para que el resfrío run its course.

It usually takes about a week for a cold to run its course.

Judy get a checkup con el doctor en el octavo piso.

Judy got a checkup with the doctor on the eighth floor.

Le llevó tres semanas al niño get over de la varicela.

It took the child three weeks to get over the chicken pox.

F ill in the blanks with the appropriate idioms.

01 Clyde's mom brought him over some chicken soup to help him _____ _____ his cold.

La madre de Clyde le llevó sopa de pollo para ayudarlo a recuperarse del resfrío.

02 Jackson left a message with his boss that he was feeling _____ the _____.

Jackson le dejó un mensaje a su jefe para decirle que se sentía enfermo.

03 Jennifer was _____ _____ for a week with the flu.

Jennifer se vio forzada a descansar por una semana debido a la gripe.

04 After sleeping all morning, Paul really _____ out _____ _____ when he woke up.

Después de dormir toda la mañana, Paul realmente se sentía aturdido cuando se despertó.

05 Stew's doctor told him that after a few more months he should get a _____ _____ to reconfirm his health condition.

El doctor de Stew le dijo que después de unos meses debería hacerse un examen físico para reconfirmar su estado de salud.

06 Since she woke up with a sore throat, Amber knew she was beginning to _____ a cold.

Debido a que se despertó con dolor de garganta, Amber sabía que le estaba dando un resfrío.

07 Just when he thought he was about to be released from the hospital, Bob _____ a turn _____ _____ _____ as he developed a sudden secondary infection.

Justo cuando pensaba que le iban a dar el alta en el hospital, Bob empeoró ya que desarrolló una repentina infección secundaria.

08 For the third night in a row, Peter took his daughter's temperature to find she was still _____ a _____.

Durante tres días seguidos, Peter le tomó la temperatura a su hija para saber si aún tenía temperatura alta.

09 The doctor's orders were to drink plenty of fluids and let the fever _____ _____ _____.

Las indicaciones del doctor fueron tomar abundante líquido y dejar que la fiebre siga su curso.

10 Norman remembered to take his vitamins since there was a virus _____ _____.

Norman recordó tomar sus vitaminas ya que había un virus contagioso/circulando.

11 Once Wesson's throat began to get sore, she could feel a cold _____ _____.

Una vez que la garganta de Wesson comenzó a irritarse sintió que se enfermaría.

12 Carol called the office early to let her boss know she would be absent because she was _____ _____ a _____.

Carol llamó a la oficina temprano para notificar a su jefe que no iría porque se sentía extremadamente enferma.

13 After working overtime every day for two weeks, Derek really felt _____ _____. He was totally exhausted.

Después de trabajar horas extras todos los días durante dos semanas Derek se sintió realmente agotado y completamente exhausto.

Answers 1. get over 2. under (the) weather 3. laid up 4. felt (out) of it 5. (get a) check up 6. catch (a cold) 7. took (a turn) for the worse 8. running (a) fever 9. run its course 10. going around 11. (a cold) coming on 12. sick as (a) dog 13. (felt) run down

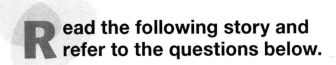

Read the following story and refer to the questions below.

- Missing Work

Amy didn't like feeling out of it. Being a senior medical student couldn't keep her from running a fever. She had gone into the hospital to do her rounds* before while she was under the weather, but this was different.

This wasn't just her feeling a cold coming on. She had known that the flu was going around, and she tried her best to protect herself from it, but got it anyway. She knew that the best thing for her to do was let the fever run its course. She had read about plenty of people that tried to go back to work too early after coming down with something like she had. Sometimes, these people would take a turn for the worse because they hated being laid up and didn't give their bodies time to get over the illness.

Amy always gave the same advice to people that came into the hospital when they were not feeling well. She would tell people to drink plenty of fluids*, get a lot of rest, and make an appointment to get a checkup the following week. So she finally called the hospital to let them know she was sick as a dog and wouldn't be in.

*rounds rondas *fluids líquidos

Questions about the story

1. How does Amy feel?
2. Is this the first time that she has worked while feeling under the weather?
3. What was going around?
4. What is the best thing that Amy can do for her condition?
5. What might happen if she doesn't get enough rest?
6. What did she finally decide to do?
7. How sick is Amy?

Questions for discussion

1. How often do you get sick?
2. When was the last time that you caught the flu and became sick as a dog?
3. Why would a cold take a turn for the worse?
4. How often do you go to the doctor to get a checkup?
5. What is the best way to get over a cold?
6. What do you do if you are laid up with an illness at home?
7. If you feel out of it, what are some things that you should or shouldn't do?

Faltar al trabajo

A Amy no le gustaba sentirse enferma. Ser una estudiante del último año de medicina no evitaría que se contagie de gripe. Ya había ido antes al hospital a hacer sus rondas* sintiéndose enferma, pero esto era diferente.

Lo que sentía no era solo un resfrío. Se había enterado de que la gripe estaba circulando e intentó todo lo posible para protegerse, pero de todas maneras le dio gripe. Sabía que lo mejor que podía hacer era dejar que la fiebre pasase. Había leído sobre mucha gente que trató de volver al trabajo demasiado pronto después de haber contraído algo como lo que ella tenía. A veces, esta gente empeoraba porque odiaban estar en cama y no dejaban que sus cuerpos tuvieran el tiempo suficiente para recuperarse de la enfermedad.

Amy siempre le daba el mismo consejo a la gente que venía al hospital cuando no se sentía bien. Les decía que tomen abundante líquido*, descansen mucho y pidan una cita para hacerse un examen médico la semana siguiente. Por esta razón, finalmente decidió llamar al hospital para decirles que estaba demasiado enferma y que no iría al trabajo.

Trouble & Ease

open (up) a can of worms
to cause or create problems that
previously did not exist.
causar o crear problemas que no
existían anteriormente.

Tammy open up a can of worms **cuando mencionó que su marido perdió su trabajo frente a toda su familia.**

Tammy opened up a can of worms when she mentioned that her husband lost his job in front of his entire family.

*This idiom is often linked to sensitive topics where a speaker misspeaks, causing the problem.
Esta expresión idiomática está a menudo relacionada con temas delicados donde una persona habla indebidamente causando problemas.

be a no-brainer
to be something quite simple,
requiring little thought.
algo demasiado simple que
requiere pensar poco; algo que
requiere poco esfuerzo.

La tarea de matemáticas de Ryan be a no-brainer. **La terminó en cinco minutos.**

Ryan's math homework was a no-brainer. He finished it in five minutes.

run into trouble
to encounter problems or difficulties.
toparse con problemas o
dificultades.
Synonym hit a snag; run into
a brick wall.

Joe run into trouble **cuando trató de obtener un permiso de construcción.**

Joe ran into trouble when he tried to gain a building permit.

in a jam
in the midst of a problem with
no apparent solution.
estar en medio de un problema sin
aparente solución.
Synonym in a bind.

Estuve in a jam **verdadero cuando se descompuso mi auto en mi primer día de trabajo.**

I was in a real jam when my car broke down on my first day of work.

*The adjective 'real' is often added to give emphasis.

El adjetivo 'real' es a menudo agregado para dar énfasis.

in dire straits
in a dreadful situation.
en una situación terrible.

Samantha estaba in dire straits después de que le robaran el pasaporte, el dinero y las tarjetas de crédito durante las vacaciones en Tailandia.
Samantha was in dire straits after being robbed of her passport, money and credit cards while on vacation in Thailand.

be in over one's head
to have more work or problems than one is able to deal with.
tener más trabajo o problemas de lo que uno pueda afrontar.

Alexander be in over his head pues toma clases en la universidad y trabaja a tiempo completo en la fábrica local.
Alexander is in over his head, taking classes at the university and working full time at the local factory.

without a hitch
without any kind of problem.
sin ningún tipo de problema.

La fiesta de cumpleaños sorpresa del tío Ed terminó without a hitch.
Uncle Ed's surprise birthday party went off without a hitch.
* 'Come off' or 'go off' often precedes this idiom.
'Come off' usualmente precede a este modismo.

ups and downs
the good times and bad times.
altibajos; los buenos y malos tiempos.

Cada matrimonio tiene ups and downs Es sólo cuestión de pasar lo bueno y lo malo juntos.
Every marriage has ups and downs. It is just a matter of getting through both the good and bad together.

be up against
to be facing an obstacle.
enfrentar un obstáculo.

Nuestro equipo nacional de fútbol be up against uno de los mejores equipos europeos durante las eliminatorias de la Copa del Mundo.
Our national soccer team will be up against some of the better European teams during the World Cup qualifying matches.

be a piece of cake
to be easy; to be simple.
ser fácil, simple; ser pan comido.
* **Synonym** as easy as pie.

La prueba de ciencia del día de mañana debería be a piece of cake para Jasmine ya que comenzó a estudiar con semanas de anticipación.
Tomorrow's science test should be a piece of cake for Jasmine, as she started studying for it weeks in advance.

F ill in the blanks with the appropriate idioms.

01 Tina was in _____ _____ when the bank decided to go back on their promise to provide additional funds so she wouldn't lose her house.

Tina se encontró en una situación terrible cuando el banco decidió faltar a la promesa de ofrecer fondos adicionales para que no perdiera su casa.

02 Although it cost me five hundred dollars, it seemed like it was a _____ _____ _____ for the repairman to fix the air conditioner.

Aunque me costó quinientos dólares, pareció ser muy simple para el técnico arreglar el aire acondicionado.

03 Burt was _____ _____ real _____ when he realized that he had locked his keys in his car while it was running at the local gas station.

Burt estaba en un verdadero problema cuando se dio cuenta de que había dejado las llaves en el auto encendido cuando se encontraba en la estación de servicio.

04 During my first year at university, I was _____ _____ my _____ when I took more courses than I could handle.

Durante mi primer año en la universidad tuve más problemas de los que podía afrontar cuando tomé más clases de las que podía manejar.

05 Spiderman was _____ _____ his greatest challenge ever when he had to face both the Green Goblin and Dr. Octavius at the same time.

El Hombre Araña enfrentó su mayor desafío cuando tuvo que luchar al mismo tiempo contra el Duende Verde y el Dr. Octopus.

06 The upcoming politician _____ a _____ _____ when he took a personal stance on religious issues.

El político entrante causó problemas cuando tomó una postura personal sobre temas religiosos.

07 Elections in the newly free Middle Eastern country went off _____ a _____ last month.

Las elecciones en el reciente país libre de Medio Oriente se desarrollaron sin ningún tipo de problema el mes pasado.

08 After I complained about being ticketed for not wearing a seatbelt, the police officer responded by telling me that it is a _____- _____to always wear a seatbelt when driving.

Después de haberme quejado por haber sido multado por no usar el cinturón de seguridad, el oficial de policía respondió diciéndome que requería poco esfuerzo utilizar siempre el cinturón de seguridad al manejar.

09 After finishing an amazing twenty five years of being a successful stock

trader in New York, Dalton decided to write a book about the ups
_____ _____ of the stock market during the past quarter of a
century.

Tras veinticinco años increíbles de ser un exitoso corredor de bolsa en Nueva York, Dalton decidió escribir un libro con los altibajos del mercado de valores durante el pasado cuarto de siglo.

10 The construction project _____ into _____ when workers
discovered an ancient Indian burial site while digging.

El proyecto de construcción se metió en problemas cuando los trabajadores descubrieron un antiguo entierro indio mientras excavaban.

Answers 1. (in) dire straits 2. (was a) piece of cake 3. in a (real) jam 4. (was) in over (my) head
5. (was) up against 6. opened (a) can of worms 7. without (a) hitch 8. (is a) no-brainer 9. (ups) and
downs 10. ran (into) trouble

R ead the following story and refer to the questions below.

- Rosalie's Renovations

Rosalie wanted a plan for an investment that would go off without a hitch. She thought that renting out a newly acquired property would be a no-brainer. Her friend Muriel had rented out one of her properties the summer before, and she said it was a piece of cake.

Rosalie's house had its ups and downs. It was on the lake but it was small, and the furniture was comfortable but old. It also needed some renovations* done before anyone could move in. So that she knew what she was up against, she called five different contractors* to get quotes on the job.

The first two were very expensive, and she knew she would be in over her head if she hired either of them. The third contractor took more time, but also opened up a can of worms when he pulled off some paneling and noticed some black mold. She knew her renovation plan had hit a snag because once it was brought to her attention, she had to pay to have the mold removed. Using most of her money to get rid of the mold put Rosalie in a real jam. It wasn't long before her finances were in dire straits without renters to pay the second mortgage.

*renovations renovaciones *contractor contratista

Questions about the story
1. What did Rosalie want to go off without a hitch?
2. How did Muriel describe the process of renting out a property?
3. How could you describe Rosalie's new property?
4. Why did she call contractors in?
5. Why didn't she hire the first two contractors?
6. How would you describe what the third contractor did?
7. How would you describe Rosalie's financial situation in the end?

Questions for discussion
1. Describe something that was a piece of cake for you to accomplish.
2. What was the single hardest obstacle that you have been up against?
3. How would you describe a situation where you were not able to handle your surroundings?
4. Describe a situation where you could have used the phrase: "I opened up a real can of worms."
5. Have you ever been in dire straits? When?

Las renovaciones de Rosalie

Rosalie quería un plan para una inversión que funcionara sin problemas. Pensó que sería muy fácil alquilar una propiedad recientemente adquirida. Su amiga Muriel había alquilado una de sus propiedades el verano anterior y dijo que era pan comido.

La casa de Rosalie tenía cosas buenas y malas. Estaba sobre el lago pero era pequeña, y los muebles eran cómodos aunque viejos. También necesitaba renovaciones* antes de que alguien pudiera mudarse. Fue allí que supo a lo que se estaba enfrentando y llamó a cinco contratistas* distintos para que cotizaran el trabajo.

Los dos primeros eran muy caros y sabía que tendría problemas con el presupuesto si contrataba a alguno de ellos. Le tomó más tiempo conseguir al tercer contratista, pero este desató más dificultades cuando sacó algunos paneles con moho negro. Supo que su plan de renovación se enfrentaba a un contratiempo cuando le dijeron que tendría que pagar por la remoción del moho. Utilizar la mayor cantidad de su dinero para retirar el moho puso a Rosalie en graves problemas: en poco tiempo sus finanzas empeoraron y no contaba con arrendatarios para pagar la segunda hipoteca.

Descriptions & Explanations

brand new
completely new; unused.
completamente nuevo; no usado.
Synonym state-of-the-art.

Si tuviera el dinero, preferiría comprar una casa brand-new antes que una usada.

If I had the money, I would rather buy a brand-new house than a used one.

* This idiom is hyphenated when used before a noun as an adjective.
Este modismo se utiliza con guión cuando actúa como adjetivo, delante de un sustantivo.

clear-cut
clear; easy to understand; straight-forward.
claro; fácil de entender; directo.
Synonym crystal clear; as clear as day.

El jefe de Jay tomó una decisión clear-cut sobre la cantidad aceptable de tiempo que podían tener los trabajadores para almorzar.

Jay's boss made a clear-cut decision about the acceptable amount of time the workers could have for lunch break.

first-rate
first class; unsurpassed in quality.
primera clase; insuperable en calidad.

Nos quedamos en un hotel cinco estrellas, un hotel first-rate durante nuestras vacaciones del año pasado.

We stayed at a five star, first-rate hotel during our vacation last year.

spick and span
very clean.
muy limpio.
Also spic and span

Samantha dijo que la casa debe estar spick and span antes de que llegue su suegra.

Samantha said that the house had to be spick and

span before her mother-in-law arrived.

out of this world
extraordinary; extremely special; amazing.
extraordinario; extremadamente especial; increíble.

El complejo turístico de la isla tropical era tan hermoso que solamente puede ser descrito como out of this world.
The tropical island resort was so beautiful that it can only be described as out of this world!

out of the ordinary
unusual; strange.
fuera de lo común, extraño.
Antonym run-of-the-mill.

La policía sabía que había algo out of the ordinary **con el sospechoso que estaban interrogando.**
The police knew that there was something out of the ordinary with the suspect they were questioning.

paint a picture
to describe something in a particular way.
describir algo de manera particular.

Los funcionarios del banco no paint a good picture **sobre mi situación financiera en el futuro.**
The bank officials didn't paint a good picture about my financial situation in the near future.

dog-eared
worn or tattered; the corners of pages folded down.
gastados o destrozados; estar dobladas las esquinas de las páginas.

La mayoría de los libros en la venta de objetos usados estaban gastados y dog-eared **por eso los precios eran bastante económicos.**
Most of the books at the garage sale were worn and dog-eared, so the prices were quite cheap.
*This idiom usually refers to books and other printed material.
Esta expresión idiomática se refiere a libros y otro material impreso.

be the pits
to be the lowest point; to be an all-time low; to be terrible.
ser lo más bajo ; ser lo peor; ser terrible.

Chris pensó que limpiar la cocina y sacar la basura era pesado, pero limpiar el baño be the pits.
Chris thought that cleaning the kitchen and taking out the garbage was annoying, but cleaning the toilet was the pits.

up to date
modern; the most recent.
moderno; el más reciente.
Antonym out of date; outdated.

El departamento de TI puso las computadoras de nuestra oficina up to date **instalando el software más nuevo.**
The IT department brought our office computers up to date by installing the newest software.
*This idiom is hyphenated when used before a noun as an adjective.
Esta expresión idiomática lleva guión cuando se utiliza como adjetivo, delante de un sustantivo.

F ill in the blanks with the appropriate idioms.

01 The old _____ - _____ books sold for about half the price of books in better condition at the local flea market.

En el mercado de pulgas local los libros viejos con esquinas gastadas se venden a mitad de precio en comparación con los libros en mejores condiciones.

02 Before leaving for the vacation island of Phuket, Matthew and Sunny thought that their hotel wouldn't be very good, but it was actually a _____ - _____ hotel.

Antes de partir a la isla de Phuket de vacaciones, Matthew y Sunny pensaron que el hotel no sería muy bueno, pero en realidad era un hotel de primera clase.

03 The new hospital had the most _____ - _____ - _____ equipment in the country.

El hospital nuevo tiene el equipo más moderno en el país.

04 Economic forecasters _____ a gloomy _____ about the country's growth for the next two years.

Los analistas económicos describieron en forma nada halagüeña el crecimiento del país para los próximos dos años.

05 Nothing seemed to be _____ of _____ _____ when the police arrived at the address of the 911 emergency call.

Nada pareció estar fuera de lo común cuando la policía llegó a la dirección desde donde se hizo la llamada al 911.

06 Have you tried Aunt Hillarie's apple pie? It is simply _____ _____ _____ world!

¿Has probado el pastel de manzana de la tía Hillarie? Es simplemente extraordinario.

07 Sandy always likes to keep the entire house _____ and _____ just in case she has unexpected visitors.

A Sandy siempre le gusta mantener la casa muy limpia en caso de que reciba visitas inesperadas.

08 Since the boss's position on freezing pay raises was so _____ - _____, there was no reason to continue the discussion.

Debido a que la posición del jefe en cuanto a congelar los aumentos en los pagos era tan clara no había motivo para continuar la discusión.

09 Jim and Stella just bought a _____ - _____ car with their retirement savings bonds.

Jim y Stella acaban de comprar un auto completamente nuevo con los bonos de ahorro de retiro.

10 Working all day in a factory in unhealthy conditions and with little time to rest is _____ _____.

Trabajar todo el día en una fábrica en condiciones insalubres y con poco tiempo para descansar es lo peor que puede existir.

Answers 1. dog-eared 2. first-rate 3. up-to-date 4. painted (a gloomy) picture 5. out (of) the ordinary 6. out of this (world) 7. spick (and) span 8. clear-cut 9. brand-new 10. (is) the pits

R ead the following story and refer to the questions below.

- Library Update

The library was the pits and everyone knew it. It was a place no one seemed interested in visiting. If they were going to keep it running, the three managers knew they had to do something soon. They interviewed people for the librarian position and, out of all of the candidates, Sarah was the clear-cut choice for the job. Her resume was out of this world and spoke for itself.*

Sarah had turned three other libraries into smooth-running operations. In her interview, she spoke about her ideas and was able to paint a picture in the minds of all three managers. Her vision was of a first-rate facility kept spick and span by a crew of volunteers whom she would bring in, and scores of* brand-new, bestselling books. She ensured the managers that the collection of books would be kept up-to-date through an automated ordering program, which she herself would install.

The managers were thrilled with Sarah's vigor* and enthusiasm*. These were qualities that they had not seen in the first eight candidates. They knew that their library needed something out of the ordinary to set it apart* from the rest in the city. Some of the other eight candidates even came with dog-eared or incomplete resumes. "How could they care for books, if that was how they cared for their resumes?" they thought.

---

*speak for itself hablar por sí mismo
*scores of montones, decenas   *vigor vigor
*enthusiasm entusiasmo   *set it apart diferenciarse

Questions about the story

1. Why did the managers feel they needed to hire someone?
2. Which position were the managers hiring for?
3. What was Sarah's vision for the library?
4. What would Sarah have the volunteers do?
5. What were the managers thrilled with?
6. Why did the managers need something out of the ordinary?
7. What was the condition of some of the other candidate's resumes?

Questions for discussion

1. What kind of picture would you paint of your own future?
2. Talk about something that you would think is out of this world.
3. What job would you consider to be the pits?
4. What places should always be kept spick and span?
5. Can you name three first-rate restaurants that are not in local hotels?
6. What is some clear-cut advice that you would give to a person younger than you?

Modernización de la biblioteca

La biblioteca era de lo peor y todos lo sabían. Era un lugar que a nadie le interesaba visitar. Si la iban a mantener en funcionamiento, los tres directores sabían que debían hacer algo pronto. Entrevistaron a gente para el puesto de bibliotecario y de todos los postulantes, Sarah fue la opción más clara para el trabajo. Su currículo era impresionante y hablaba por sí mismo.*

Sarah había puesto en funcionamiento otras tres bibliotecas. En su entrevista, habló sobre sus ideas y pudo describirlas detalladamente para que los directores comprendieran lo que quería hacer. Su visión era instalar una biblioteca de primera clase mantenida de manera perfecta por un equipo de voluntarios que ella iba a traer y contar con montones de libros completamente nuevos y populares. Ella les aseguró a los directores que la selección de libros sería mantenida y actualizada a través de un programa automático de pedidos que ella misma instalaría.

Los directores estaban emocionados con el vigor* y entusiasmo* de Sarah. Estas eran las cualidades que no habían visto en los primeros ocho postulantes. Ellos sabían que la biblioteca necesitaba algo fuera de lo ordinario para diferenciarse* del resto de bibliotecas de la ciudad. Algunos de los ocho postulantes hasta se presentaron con currículos con las páginas dobladas o incompletas. "¿Cómo podían cuidar los libros si así cuidaban sus currículos personales?", pensaron.

Chapters ㉑ - ㉕

Review Chapters 21-25 and fill in the crossword below.

Answers → P.173

Across

04. Bill decided to relax at home on his vacation this year rather than _____ _____.

06. The construction project _____ _____ trouble when the building permits didn't come through.

08. I hate waiting for the bus, so I _____ _____ by deleting old text messages.

11. Ken thought the math test was a piece _____ _____, but everyone else said it was too hard.

12. Be sure to wear a hat and coat outside today or you will _____ a cold.

13. OK, my room is _____ and _____, but don't look in the closet.

15. Ted opened up a _____ _____ _____ when he started praising God at the atheist convention.

18. On weekends, Kelly loves to _____ around the house with a good book.

19. My copy of War and Peace is _____ - _____ from reading it so much.

21. They decided to _____ a flight to Hawaii for their honeymoon.

22. Sam was _____ _____ _____ when he locked his keys in his car, so he broke a window to get in.

23. Are you sick? Be careful; the flu is _____ around.

Down

01. Jon is going to _____ some time _____ from work to go see the Olympics.

02. The Minister is _____ a gloomy _____ about the unemployment rate.

03. Even though Patrick felt sick, he wasn't _____ a fever.

05. He goes to his cabin to _____ _____ and relax.

06. It usually takes about a week for a cold to _____ _____ _____.

07. Will wanted to _____ _____ all the sights in Athens, so he spent a week looking around.

09. Erin just lost her _____ - _____ cell phone and has to buy another one.

10. She thought opening a coffee shop would be a _____ - _____, but it was a lot of work.

14. The new hospital had the most _____ - _____ - _____ equipment in the country.

15. We decided to wait out the long line to _____ _____ at the hotel with a drink in the lobby.

16. After a week in the desert, everyone in the expedition was feeling _____ _____.

17. Ryan is working too hard. I think he needs to _____ up.

20. Peter had to wait for his friends so he listened to music to _____ the time.

Index

A

ace	49
after hours	28
al of a sudden	35
ASAP	33
as easy as pie	157
as far as	59
a sight for sore eyes	91
ask someone out	132
as soon as	33
at once	33
at the last minute	34

B

be a no-brainer	156
be a piece of cake	157
beat around the bush	98
be booked up	144
be free	131
be from	114
be in over one's head	157
be laid up	151
be my guest	127
be news to someone	103
be rained out	78
be sold out (of)	53
be the pits	162
be under the weather	150
be up against	157
black sheep	115
blind date	121
blurt out	98
book something	145
bookworm	48
brand new	161

break it off	119
break the ice	90
break up 109,	119
breakup	119
bring up	115
broaden one's horizons	102
brush up (on)	47
bumper-to-bumper	60
buy up	55

C

call someone back	85
call (someone) up	83
carryout	66
catch a cold	151
catch you later	92
cat got your tongue	98
check in	144
check into	144
check out (of)	144
chill: to relax (slang)	138
clam up	98
clean house	72
clean out	73
clean up	71
clear-cut	161
clear up	39
cloud up	39
cold snap	41
cold spell	41
come about	17
come down in sheets	40
come down with (a cold)	151
come from	114
come over	125

come to an end	17
come to pass	16
come up	79
cool down	40
cool off	40
crack of dawn	21
cram	47
crank call	85
crash	29
crash out	29
crave for	66
crazy weather	41
crystal clear	161
cut class; cut school; play hooky	49

D

daydream	137
die down	40
dog-eared	162
doggy bag	66
do the dishes	72
down the road	35
draw to a close	17
drop by	125
drop in on	125
drop out	49
dry up	40

E

eat out	65
eat up	67
ex-boyfriend	120, 121
ex-girlfriend	121

F

face to face	109
fall asleep	28
fall through	79
feel a cold coming on	151
feel/be run down	151
feel out of it	150
fender bender	61
finish off	16
fire away	97
first-rate	161
fix up	72, 120
flesh and blood	114

flunk out	48
for a fact	102
from scratch	16

G

garage sale	72
get a checkup	152
get along with	108
get back	145
get cut off	84
get dumped	120
get forty winks	137
get in someone's face	108
get oneself/someone going	23
get one's message across	98
get over	152
get ready	22
get the ball rolling	17
get together	109, 126
get-together	126
get up	21
get up on the wrong side of the bed	23
get wind of	103
give birth to	114
give someone a call	83
go along (with)	132
go away	144
going around	151
go off	21, 78
go on sale	54
go out	28
go out on a date	119
go out with	119
go sightseeing	145
go steady	120
go to bed	28
go to sleep	28
grab a bite	65
grab a seat	126
gridlock	61
grow up	114
gulp down	66

H

hand down	115
hand in	48
hand-me-down	115

handout	48	in the short term	35
hang a left/right	59		
hang up	84	**J**	
hang up on someone	84	junk food	66
has the cat got your tongue	98	just about to	34
hat's going on?	92		
have a boy	114	**K**	
have a craving for	66	keep house	73
have a girl	114	kick back	138
have a seat	126	kick off	16
have a sweet tooth	67	killer weather	41
have a way with words	98	kill time	138
have free time	138	knockout	120
have not seen someone for ages	91	know-how	102
have not seen someone in a dog's age	91		
have someone over	131	**L**	
have the gift of gab	98	leftovers	65
have time off	143	let one's hair down	139
have time on one's hands	138	let up	40
hear of	102	like father	115
heat up	40	like son	115
heat wave	40	long time no see	92
hit a snag; run into a brick wall	156	loosen up	139
hit it off (with someone)	108	lounge around	138
hit the books	47		
hit the hay	29	**M**	
hit the sack	29	make a call	83
hold an event	78	make a prank call	85
hold it down	97	make a U-turn	60
hold on	84	make a wrong turn	60
hot	120	make breakfast; make lunch; make dinner;	
how about	131	make a snack	72
hunt for bargains	54	make food	72
		make friends	108
I		make of	103
ice-breaker	90	make oneself at home	127
in a bind	156	make oneself feel at home	127
in a flash	35	make out	119
in a heartbeat	34	make small talk	90
in a jam	156	make someone feel at home	126
in a jiffy	33	make up	121
in dire straits	157	morning breath	22
in no time	33		
in the know	103	**N**	
in the long run	34	nod off; doze off	28
in the long term	35	not miss a beat	34
in the loop	103	not sleep a wink	22

O

odds and ends	72
off the cuff	98
off the hook	84
off the phone	83
off the top of one's head	98
old flame	120, 121
on leave	143
on sale	54
on the hook	84
on the line. En línea	83
on the phone	83
on the rocks	109
open (up) a can of worms	156
out of date; outdated.	162
out of the loop	103
out of the ordinary	162
out of this world	162
over the phone	85

P

paint a picture	162
pass the time	139
pay a visit	126
pea soup fog	41
(a) penny for your thoughts	97
pick out	54
pick up 53, 71,	103
pig out	66
pop quiz	47
potluck	66
powwow	115
pull into	60
pull over	60
put away	73
put on hold	84
put something back	73

R

rain buckets	39
rain cats and dogs	39
rain check	55
rain out.rain out	78
right away	34
rub elbows with	109
rub shoulders with	109
run a fever	150

run a (red) light	59
run into trouble	156
run its course	152
run-of-the-mill	162

S

see someone off	143
see someone out	127
see you around	92
sellout	79
settle down	115
set up	120
shake hands	91
shoot someone down	132
shoot the breeze	90
shoot the shit	90
shop around	53
show someone in	125
sick as a dog	151
sightseeing	145
sign up	48
skip school	49
sleep in	21
sleep like a log	22
sleepyhead	22
snap up	54
so far	33
so far, so good	33
speak one's mind	97
spic and span	161
spick and span	161
spitting	41
split up	109, 110
split up	119
spring cleaning	73
stand someone up	119
start off on the right foot	110
start off on the wrong foot	110
start the ball rolling	17
start the day off right	22
state-of-the-art	161
stay in	27
stay out	27
stay up	27
sticky weather	41
stock up (on)	54
stop and go	60

stopover	125	**V**		
stop over to visit for a period of time	125	visit with		126
straighten up	71			
strike up a conversation	90	**W**		
swing by	126	wait up		27
		wake up		21
T		wake up call		144
tag along	132	what's happening?		92
take a break	138	what's new		92
take a breather	138	what's shakin?		92
take a chair	126	what's up		92
take after	115	window shop		53
take a load off	138	without a doubt		34
take a nap	137	without a hitch		157
take a rain check	131	without missing a beat		34
take a turn for the worse	150	wolf down		66
take back	55			
take care	92	**Y**		
take in	144	yard sale		73
take in the sights	145			
take it easy	137			
take out	66, 71			
takeout	65			
take place	78			
take someone up on something	132			
take (time) off	145			
teacher's pet	48			
through the grapevine	103			
tidy up	71			
tie the knot	109			
time to kill	138			
tired out	28			
turn around	59			
turn away	79			
turn down	132			
turn in	28, 48			
turn out (for)	79			
turn over a new leaf	17			
U				
(not over) until the fat lady sings	17			
upkeep	73			
ups and downs	157			
up to date	162			
up to speed	59			
usher in	16			

Crossword Answers

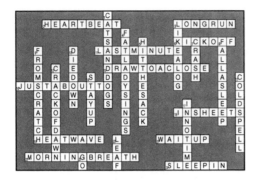

Chapters ❶ - ❺

Across

2. HEARTBEAT 3. LONGRUN 6. KICKOFF
11. LASTMINUTE 13. DRAWTOACLOSE
16. JUSTABOUTTO 18. INSHEETS 19. HEATWAVE
21. WAITUP 22. MORNINGBREATH 24. SLEEPIN

Down

1. CATSANDDOGS 3. LIKEALOG 4. FATLADYSINGS
5. HITTHESACK 7. CRASH 8. FALLASLEEP
9. FROMSCRATCH 10. DIEDOWN
12. CRACKOFDAWN 14. STAYUP 15. COLDSPELL
17. INNOTIME 20. LEAF 23. GO

Chapters ❻ - ❿

Across

1. WINDOWSHOP 10. SPRINGCLEANING
12. CLEANOUT 13. POP 14. INTO 15. RAINCHECK
16. WOLFDOWN 20. DOTHEDISHES 22. HUNTFOR
23. DOGGYBAG 24. JUNKFOOD 25. GRABABITE

Down

2. ODDSANDENDS 3. PICK 4. RANALIGHT
5. TAKEOUT 6. HITTHEBOOKS 7. FENDERBENDER
8. TEACHERSPET 9. DROPPEDOUT
11. GETACRAVING 17. PULLOVER 18. FLUNKED
19. STOCKUP 21. STOPGO

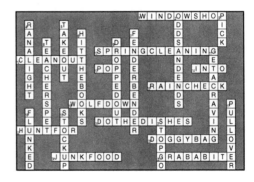

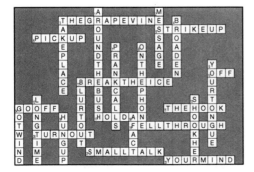

Chapters ⓫ - ⓯

Across

3. THEGRAPEVINE 5. STRIKEUP 6. PICKUP
10. OFF 11. BREAKTHEICE 14. GOOFF
15. THEHOOK 17. HOLDAN 19. FELLTHROUGH
20. TURNOUT 21. SMALLTALK 22. YOURMIND

Down

1. AROUNDTHEBUSH 2. MESSAGE 3. TAKEPLACE
4. BROADEN 7. PRANKCALLS 8. ONTHEPHONE
9. YOURTONGUE 11. BLURTOUT 12. LONGTIME
13. SHOOKHER 14. GOTWIND 16. HUNGUP
18. AFACT

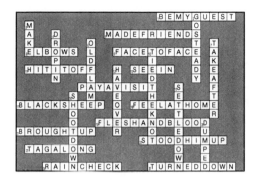

Chapters 16 - 20

Across
1. BEMYGUEST 5. MADEFRIENDS 8. ELBOWS
9. FACETOFACE 11. HITITOFF 13. SEEIN
14. PAYAVISIT 17. BLACKSHEEP 18. FEELATHOME
19. FLESHANDBLOOD 21. BROUGHTUP
22. STOODHIMUP 23. TAGALONG 24. RAINCHECK
25. TURNEDDOWN

Down
2. GOSTEADY 3. MAKE 4. DROPIN 6. OLDFLAME
7. TAKEAFTER 10. TIEDTHEKNOT 12. HAVEOVER
15. SETTLEDOWN 16. SHOOTDOWN 20. DUMPED

Chapters 21 - 25

Across
4. GOAWAY 6. RANINTO 8. KILLTIME 11. OFCAKE
12. CATCH 13. SPICKSPAN 15. CANOFWORMS
18. LOUNGE 19. DOGEARED 21. BOOK 22. INAJAM
23. GOING

Down
1. TAKEOFF 2. PAINTINGPICTURE 3. RUNNING
5. KICKBACK 6. RUNITSCOURSE 7. TAKEIN
9. BRANDNEW 10. NOBRAINER 14. UPTODATE
15. CHECKIN 16. RUNDOWN 17. LOOSEN
20. PASS

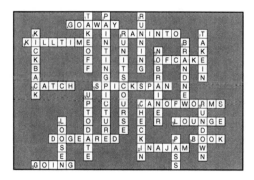

Dedication & Copyright

⌐ This book is dedicated to the love of language,

to the warp of words & twisted meaning

and to the art of deciphering them. ⌐

ISBN 978-0-9801974-6-4
eBook ISBN 978-1-936342-04-4
Idiom Attack 1: Everyday Living – Spanish edition

Exile Press LLC
2355 Fairview Avenue North, #191
Roseville, MN 55113

Library of Congress Cataloging-in-Publication Data
Liptak, Peter N.
Idiom Attack / by Peter N. Liptak, Matt Douma & Jay Douma. 1st ed.
p.176 cm. 24.4
Includes Table of Contents and Index
Library of Congress Control Number : 2010939941
ISBN 978-0-9801974-6-4 (alk. paper)
1. English language – Idioms 2. Spanish language 3. Americanisms
4. English language – Terms and phrases – dictionaries – Spanish.
I. Title
LC Classification: PE1689 .L57 2010
Language Code: engspa

ɛxile pɾess

Exile Press LLC
www.ExilePress.com

CPSIA information can be obtained at www.ICGtesting.com

226893LV00003B/18/P

9 780980 197464